What People Are Saying About
Chicken Soup for the College Soul . . .

"Many of my most vivid memories and challenges happened during my college years at the University of Oklahoma. The mechanics of achievement that I learned have helped me move from being a student-athlete to an Olympic Champion and an achiever in the so-called 'real world.' *Chicken Soup for the College Soul* focuses on the critical years when we are setting the path for our future. I am sure readers will be inspired by the touching anecdotes that have made the *Chicken Soup* series so successful. I give it a 10.0!"

Bart Conner
1984 Olympic Gold Medal gymnast
sports commentator

"*Chicken Soup for the College Soul* is the hottest hit on college campuses today."

Rick Dees
Rick Dees Weekly Top 40

"If you enjoyed my story of my experience at Notre Dame, you will love the stories in *Chicken Soup for the Soul*."

Rudy Ruettiger
of the Tri-Star motion picture, *Rudy*

"As a former college administrator for twenty-two years and the current executive director of an association focused on development issues for college students, I can recommend *Chicken Soup for the College Soul* as a valuable resource for students and parents. These inspiring stories provide insight into the types of learning so important to students as they prepare for life beyond college."

Alan B. Davis
executive director, National Association for Campus Activities

"Absolutely amazing! College is such a critical time in one's life journey, and this book inspires, empowers, and guides anyone in college or entering college. This book has encouraged me to never give up on my dreams, no matter what."

Elizabeth Randazzese
president, Student Government Association
junior, Rowan University

"I attribute my success as a family man, football player and businessman to the inspirational principles found in *Chicken Soup for the College Soul*. I highly recommend this book to all young people everywhere."

Roger Staubach
chairman and CEO, The Staubach Company
Heisman Trophy winner, 1963
NFL Hall of Fame Quarterback, 1985
Super Bowl MVP

"College is such a unique time and can be such a uniquely wonderful time if a student is inspired to make the most of it. *Chicken Soup for the College Soul* brings to life—sometimes poignantly, sometimes pointedly and sometimes pleasurably— that the fullest trip through college is a wide-ranging exploration of curricular, extracurricular and personal opportunities."

Gregory F. Hauser, Esq.
president, National Interfraternity Conference

"I am so glad to see the *Chicken Soup* series expanded to include college students. In fact, I first heard about these books from one of my own children, a college freshman. These are fun and happy books that help all of us in our daily need for practical wisdom and inspiration. I gladly recommend this newest book for the college student."

Dr. Robert B. Sloan Jr.
president, Baylor University

"These heartfelt stories remind me how truly generous, caring, and dedicated many college campus leaders are today! And they inspire *me*, too!"

W. H. "Butch" Oxendine Jr.
publisher and editor in chief, *Student Leader Magazine*

"The college experience, especially in today's fast-paced, technology-driven world, involves far more than what takes place in the classroom. *Chicken Soup for the College Soul* is not just a collection of stories; it is a compilation of the many experiences that students endure as they progress through this oftentimes challenging period in their lives. Some of those experiences are inspirational and moving, others simply amusing and entertaining. This book, no doubt, could be a valuable companion throughout a student's entire collegiate career, providing incentive, motivation, and reassurance that everything will work out."

James H. McCormick
chancellor, Pennsylvania State System of Higher Education

"This latest *Chicken Soup* publication is a very readable and poignant reminder that the individuals who benefit the most from college are the ones who are open to new experiences and appreciate people who are different from them. This is must reading for college students of all ages."

Paul M. Oliaro
vice president for Student Affairs, West Chester University

"I read this book toward the end of my freshman year at college. I laughed so hard (and cried, too) that my roommates thought I was crazy. Before long they insisted that I read the stories out loud so they could share in the laughter (or tears)."

Lia Gay
student, University of Kansas

"College is so stressful and so often you just want to get in bed and pull the covers over your head. Curling up with this book is the perfect medicine for 'a day in the life of a college student.'"

Matt Boucher
college student

"This book captures the true essence of the college experience. *Chicken Soup for the College Soul* shares touching and inspirational stories about the most important lessons learned in college, the ones outside the classroom. *Chicken Soup for the College Soul* is a must-have during this pivotal stage in personal development called 'college.'"

Jeremy Louis Harman
director, Conference on Student Government Associations
student, Texas A&M University

"My college days were so filled with the unknown and the unexpected. Even after taking a year off as Miss America between my sophomore and junior years, I would still constantly worry about the wisdom of my decisions, the disappointment of new failures and the knowledge that giving up wasn't an option. College was a concentrated time for my young mind to learn how to react to challenge . . . and to teach myself in practicality the old saying, 'Success is never final, and failure is never fatal.' *Chicken Soup for the College Soul* inspires students to not just *survive* college, but to feast on the character-defining moments unique to the college experience."

Sharlene Hawkes
former Miss America

"Some of the most moving and inspirational stories come from the experiences of college-age adults. However, your soul does not have to be college age to be touched and motivated by this extraordinary book."

Grant Teaff
executive director, American Football Coaches Association

"*Chicken Soup for the College Soul* is the perfect recipe to keep us warm and wise during life's 'winter' moments. Just a few pages and our fire is relit, propelling us forward, once again, to go back out into the world and shine!"

Cathy Lee Crosby
actress, producer
author, *Let the Magic Begin*

"*Chicken Soup for the Soul* has done it again! It reminds us that a good deed, an act of kindness or simply sharing oneself honestly with others can be life changing."

Derick Morat
director of student activities & University Center,
University of the Pacific, Stockton, California

CHICKEN SOUP
FOR THE
COLLEGE SOUL

Chicken Soup for the College Soul
Inspiring and Humorous Stories About College
Jack Canfield, Mark Victor Hansen, Kimberly Kirberger, Dan Clark, James Malinchak
Published by Backlist, LLC,
a unit of Chicken Soup for the Soul Publishing, LLC. www.chickensoup.com

Front cover redesign by Andrea Perrine Brower
Cover photo ©1999 Terry Wild Studio
Originally published in 1999 by Health Communications, Inc.

Back cover and spine redesign by Pneuma Books, LLC

Distributed to the booktrade by Simon & Schuster. SAN: 200-2442

Publisher's Cataloging-in-Publication Data
(Prepared by The Donohue Group)

Chicken soup for the college soul : inspiring and humorous stories about college / [compiled by] Jack Canfield ... [et al.].

  p. : ill. ; cm.

  Originally published: Deerfield Beach, FL : Health Communications, c1999.
  ISBN: 978-1-62361-084-5

  1. College students--Conduct of life--Anecdotes. 2. Anecdotes. I. Canfield, Jack, 1944-

BJ1661 .C26 2012
158.1/28/0842   2012944485

PRINTED IN THE UNITED STATES OF AMERICA
on acid free paper
21 20 19 18 17   03 04 05 06 07 08 09 10

CHICKEN SOUP
FOR THE
COLLEGE SOUL

Inspiring and Humorous
Stories About College

Jack Canfield
Mark Victor Hansen
Kimberly Kirberger
Dan Clark
James Malinchak

Backlist, LLC, a unit of
Chicken Soup for the Soul Publishing, LLC
Cos Cob, CT
www.chickensoup.com

Contents

3. LESSONS FROM THE CLASSROOM

4. LESSONS FROM OUTSIDE THE CLASSROOM

9. MIND OVER MATTER

10. GRADUATION

CONTENTS

Introduction

Dear College Student,

We are excited about this book. It has been a true labor of love for us, as well as a complete education in itself. In the process of creating this book we read over eight thousand stories and poems and talked to hundreds of college students. The journey has been a rewarding one. We have discovered much about today's students and we are very impressed with what we have seen and heard.

You have worked very hard to get to where you are and you seem to know the importance of the job that still awaits you. You are preparing to inherit a world with many problems; yet, it is clear to us that you have the intelligence and the heart necessary to confront and solve them.

Being all too aware of the stresses and pressures you are under, we have worked diligently to give you a book that will offer you the inspiration, motivation, insights and comic relief you will need to do the job at hand.

We have filled this book with anecdotes about the difficult transition from home to college and from adolescent to adult. There are stories about professors who inspire and students who excel. There are stories that will make you laugh and stories that contain the wisdom of those who have been there.

The college years are packed with so much emotional challenge. It has been said that people grow and develop the most during two periods of their lives: before the age of five and during college. Therefore, it is so important that you remember to be good to yourself and nourish yourself with as much *Chicken Soup* as possible during this important time of transition.

So, here you go. A book from our heart to yours. May it give you hope when you have none, may it inspire you when you most need it, and may it remind you to take things lightly and never be so serious that you forget to laugh.

We wish you love, joy, courage and the strength to persevere.

From a Previous Reader

[EDITORS' NOTE: *The following story was submitted to us by a college student about her first day on campus.*]

Common Ground

Towards the end of high school, when it came time to start thinking about what colleges I was interested in applying to, there was only one thing on my mind: I wanted to get away from home. I was the oldest of two kids, and had begun to feel the urge to be on my own, that I was ready to take charge of my own life.

Even at the time of being accepted to Virginia Tech, I was excited at the prospect of starting over, with new faces, and new things to see and do. I had no boyfriend at the time, (in fact, I had just gotten out of a pretty bad relationship), and felt that I had no ties keeping me in my New Jersey hometown.

But as the time arrived to pack my bags and prepare to leave, the reality of what I was doing hit home hard. I cried as I realized that I was going to be eight-and-a-half hours away from everything and everybody that was familiar to me. I was leaving the town where I had grown up, and all the things about it that I loved.

For the first few days after arriving at school, I thought that I was not going to make it through the year. I had yet to meet anyone besides a few random girls in my dorm, whom I was fairly sure did not even remember my name. After a tearful call back home, I grabbed one of the few books that had make it into my suitcase, *Chicken Soup for the Teenage Soul,* and I headed down to the quad to read a few stories. They had always been able to cheer me up before, and I was hopeful that they would now.

On the way out, I passed another girl in the hallway. She saw the book in my hand and smiled, saying that she had the same book in her dorm room, too. I took a chance, and invited her to come read with me. Being as homesick as I was, she agreed, and we found our way onto the quad.

Before we knew it, we were surrounded by girls, who, like us, had either read or owned the book, and who loved it as much as we did. As I watched the tears fall down everyone's faces and the smiles grow as we all read, I realized that I was not alone, and even if all we had in common was the love for the book, it was something to start with.

The days went on, and I still missed home— but the campus was beautiful, the people were kind, and it became better and better as the school year continued. I began to realize that there were many people who, like myself, were homesick and just wanted to make friends. The night we spent reading bonded a group of us together, and most of us still hang out now.

The binding of my book is now ripped and cracked from overuse, but I still feel amazing when I read each story. It is unbelievable to me how many souls and hearts have been touched by the book, and how many spirits have been raised and inspired. It gave me hope for a great new beginning, and the knowledge that sometimes all it takes is one small thing for many people to find a common ground.

Megan Narcini

1

GETTING IN

*And yet not a dream, but a mighty reality—
a glimpse of the higher life, the broader
possibilities of humanity, which is granted to
the man who, amid the rush and roar of
living, pauses four short years to learn what
living means.*

W. E. B. DuBois

Reprinted by permission of Randy Glasbergen.

Never Say Never

I cannot remember a point in my life when I desired anything other than becoming a teacher. As a child, I played school with my little cousins and friends just so I could practice for my future career. But what I didn't realize as a child was how expensive my dream was. I came from a middle-class family, and it seemed as though we'd always struggled to make ends meet. My dream of attending the University of Connecticut seemed so out of reach, but I wasn't willing to settle for anything less.

In the beginning of my senior year in high school, I began applying to colleges, but in my heart I had already made my decision. The University of Connecticut was the one. But a huge hurdle stood between me and my dream—lack of financial resources.

At first, I was ready to give up. I mean, who was going to give me, the average high-school girl, that kind of money? I wasn't the smartest person in my class, not even close; but my heart was in the right place, and I was determined. I knew that scholarships were only given to the really smart kids, or so I thought. I applied for every scholarship I could get my hands on. What did I have to lose? And then my guidance counselor told me about the financial aid system. I applied, but I didn't think I would qualify for that either.

After the holidays, my friends started receiving their acceptance letters from colleges, and I eagerly anticipated mine. Finally, a letter arrived from the University of Connecticut. Feelings of fear and joy overwhelmed me, but I was ready. I opened the envelope with trembling hands as tears engulfed my eyes. I had done it! I had been accepted to the University of Connecticut! I cried for a while, feeling both extremely excited and afraid. I had worked so hard to get accepted; what if I was denied admission because of my financial status?

I had been working a full-time job, but that was barely enough to pay for tuition. My parents couldn't afford that kind of money, and I wasn't going to pretend that they could. I was the first person in my family who would attend a university, and I knew how proud my parents were; but it was impossible for them to finance my education. However, my parents are incredible people, and they taught me never to give up on my dreams, regardless of the obstacles that I encounter, and never to lose sight of what I truly want out of life. My parents were right, and I continued to believe in both myself and my dreams.

Months went by before I heard anything from the financial aid office. I assumed that I didn't qualify for aid, but I wasn't ready to lose hope yet. At last, a letter arrived. I opened it eagerly, but it was a false alarm. The letter requested more information in order to process my application.

This happened over and over, and my hopes kept getting shot down. Finally, a bulky envelope arrived. I knew this was the one that would determine whether or not I could attend college. I opened the envelope and could hardly understand what any of the documents inside meant.

The following day, I brought the documents to school and asked my guidance counselor to take a look at them. He looked up at me with a huge smile on his face and told me that not only was financial aid going to help me out with my expenses, but I had also won two of the scholarships I had applied for! I was in shock at first, then I cried. I had actually made my dream come true.

I am now a junior at the University of Connecticut, pursuing a degree in English. In the beginning of the new millennium, my dream will become a reality. I will be a teacher.

I live by this quote: "Reach for the sky because if you should happen to miss, you'll still be among the stars."

Rosa Torcasio

College Bound

My son is a senior in high school, which means that pretty soon he, like millions of other seniors, will have to make a crucial decision, the consequences of which will remain with him for the rest of his life: Who will be his prom date?

Also, at some point he'll probably select a college. In fact, we've already gone on several college visits, which are helpful in choosing a college because you can get answers to important academic questions such as:

- Is there parking?
- Are all the students required to get body piercings? Or is this optional at the undergraduate level?
- Is there a bank near the college that you can rob to pay the tuition?

Most college visits include an orientation session, wherein you sit in a lecture room and a college official tells you impressive statistics about the college, including, almost always, how small the classes are. Class smallness is considered the ultimate measure of how good a college is. Harvard, for example, has zero students per class: The professors just sit alone in their classrooms, filing their nails.

I noticed, in these orientation sessions, that many of the kids seem semi-bored, whereas the parents not only take notes, but also ask most of the questions, sometimes indicating that they've mapped out their children's entire academic careers all the way through death. There will be some girl who looks like she's eleven years old, and her dad will raise his hand and say: "If my daughter declares a quadruple major in Biology, Chemistry, Physics and Large Scary Equations, and she graduates with honors and then earns doctorates in Medicine, Engineering, Law, Architecture, Dentistry and Taxidermy, and then she qualifies for a Merwanger Fellowship for Interminable Postdoctoral Studies, does the Nobel organization pay her expenses to Sweden to pick up her prize?"

I was intimidated by these parents. I have frankly not given that much thought to my son's academic goals. I assumed he was going to college for the same reason I did, which is that at some point they stop letting you go to high school. I tried to think of questions to ask the college officials, but the only one I could think of was: "How come these lecture-hall desks are never designed for us left-handed people?" Although I didn't ask this, because it's probably considered insensitive on college campuses to say "left-handed people." You probably have to say something like "persons of handedness."

After the orientation session, you go on a campus tour conducted by a student who is required to tell you the name of every single building on the campus, no matter how many there are ("Over there is the Gwendolyn A. Heckenswacker Institute for the Study of Certain Asian Mollusks, which we call 'The Heck.' And over there is the Myron and Gladys B. Prunepocket Center for Musty Old Books That Nobody Ever Looks At. And right next to that is The Building Right Next to the Myron and Gladys . . ."). After the tour, the kids have interviews with college officials. My son revealed little about what goes on in these interviews. My theory is that the officials close the door and say: "Relax. You'll spend the majority of college attending parties, playing hacky sack and watching *Friends*. The tour is purely for the parents. The guides make up the building names as they go along."

One of the colleges my son visited was my alma mater, Haverford College (proud motto: "Among The First In The Nation To Drop Football"). I was a little nervous about going back: I expected that, at any moment, the dean would tap me on the shoulder and say: "Mr. Barry, we need to talk to you about your share of the Class of 1969's bill for the cost of scraping an estimated twenty-three thousand butter pats off the dining-hall ceiling."

Fortunately, this did not happen. Our student guide gave an excellent tour, although he failed to point out some of the more historic sites at Haverford, including:

- The building where, in 1967, the rock band "The Federal Duck" made the historic discovery that if it was going to play "Purple Haze" correctly, it needed WAY bigger amplifiers;
- The dormitory room where my roommate Bob Stern and I accumulated what historians believe was the world's largest man-made pile of unlaundered briefs.

Those are my most vivid memories, although I also vaguely recall attending classes and learning numerous English-major facts that still come in mighty handy whenever the topic of conversation turns—as it so often does—to Seventeenth-Century English metaphysical poetry. Yes, college was a valuable experience for me, and I'm sure it will also be one for my son, wherever he decides to go. On prom night, I mean.

Dave Barry

Bloopers from College Admission Essays

Caught up in the hurly-burly, helter-skelter and hugger-mugger of college applications, a student aspiring to enter Bates College once wrote, "I am in the mist of choosing colleges." The admissions departments at Bates and Vassar Colleges have compiled a list of bloopers from their admissions essays:

- If there was a single word to describe me, that word would have to be "profectionist."
- I was abducted into the national honor society.
- In my senior year, I am serving as writting editor of the yearbook.
- I want to be bilingual in three or more languages.
- I have made the horror role every semester.
- I want a small liberal in the northeast part of the country.
- Bates is a college I can excell in.
- I am writing to tell you that I was very discouraged when I found out that I had been differed from Bates.

- I am thinking of possibly transferring to your college. I applied as an undergraduate but was weight listed.
- I first was exposed through a friend who attends Vassar.
- I would love to attend a college where the foundation was built upon women.
- My mother worked hard to provide me with whatever I needed in my life, a good home, a stale family and a wonderful education.
- Playing the saxophone lets me develop technique and skill which will help me in the future, since I would like to become a doctor.
- Such things as divorces, separations and annulments greatly reduce the need for adultery to be committed.
- I am proud to be able to say that I have sustained from the use of drugs, alcohol and tobacco products.
- I've been a strong advocate of the abomination of drunk driving.
- Activities: Cook and serve homeless.
- Another activity I take personally is my church Youth Group.
- He was a modest man with an unbelievable ego.
- The worst experience that I have probably ever had to go through emotionally was when other members of PETA (People for the Ethical Treatment of Animals) and I went to Pennsylvania for their annual pigeon shooting.

Now it is clear why one candidate wrote in his or her admissions essay, "I would like to see my own ignorance wither into enlightenment."

Richard Lederer

Strange Scholarships

Want some help with college tuition? You might qualify for one of these scholarships. In 1994, it was announced that:

- The Frederick & Mary F. Beckley Fund for Needy Left-handed Freshman offers up to $1,000 for left-handers who want to go to Juanita College in Pennsylvania.
- The National Make It Yourself with Wool scholarship offers $100–$1,000 to knitters.
- The Dolphin Scholarship Foundation offers $1,750 to the children of WWII submarine veterans.
- The John Gatling Scholarship Program offers $6,000 to anyone with the last name Gatlin or Gatling who wants to go to the University of North Carolina.
- Tall Clubs International offers two scholarships of $1,000 each for females 5'10" or taller, and males 6'2" or taller.

Uncle John's Great Big Bathroom Reader

The Envelope, Please

The people who get on in this world are the people who get up and look for the circumstances they want, and if they can't find them, make them.

George Bernard Shaw

When I found out I didn't get into the colleges I wanted to go to, I was in New York City on a school trip. I called home from a pay phone, and my little sister, Alex, said four envelopes had arrived: Georgetown, Cornell, William and Mary and the University of Massachusetts. She then opened and read them to me in her adenoidal, ten-year-old voice: "We regret that we do not have a place for you. . . ." Rejected from Georgetown. "You were one of many qualified candidates. . . ." Rejected from Cornell. And number seventy-three on a waiting list of seventy-five at William and Mary. Accepted to U Mass, my safety school.

I didn't digest the rejections immediately. I toured the United Nations, took Amtrak home and went back to school. Then I realized that other people had gotten into schools they really wanted to go to. Up to that point in my seventeen years, I hadn't really failed at anything. I got good grades, made varsity and scored well on my SATs. I hadn't experienced any major disappointments in my life—no deaths, no disease, no divorce, no cavities even. So being rejected seemed apocalyptic.

I had always assumed I'd go to one of the "good schools." I really wanted to be chosen: This is the place for smart people, and we want you. U Mass, on the other hand, had the reputation of being a party school—to which, come September, I'd be headed with the guy who sat next to me in tenth-grade history and who, during tests, left his book open on the floor and flipped through it with his feet.

I became bitter. I compared everyone's grades and talents to my own in a desperate attempt to make my own misfortune add up. "Of course she got into Harvard. Her dad went there. Who needs a frontal lobe when you're a legacy?" I was melodramatic. Talking to teachers, relatives or friends, I'd say, "I'm going to U Mass," projecting my indignation onto them. *Not U Mass,* I'd imagine them thinking. *Not you.* I'd draw a deep breath, raise my eyebrows and frown slightly, like some old Yankee farmer confirming the death of a faithful plow-ox.

I did not get proactive like my friend Heather, who, having been rejected by her first choice, made *I Love Lucy-*style plans to drive to the Duke campus with her soccer ball and her science-fair project to show the admissions board exactly what they were rejecting. I simply adopted the mantra, "I'll transfer after one semester." And I'd say things like, "I've decided to forego the bachelor's degree and take a cake-decorating course." The subtext in all these conversations was: I'm stupid. The world isn't fair. I made my jokes right up to the registration desk in my dorm, where I had my little sister present my paperwork and pretend to be me.

The strangest thing happened, though: I liked U Mass. I met Marci, my soul mate, whose first choice had also been Cornell. However, U Mass had been her second. Finally I'd found someone who would take a nightly three-mile jog with me to buy a sundae. And I met lots of other smart, funny, interesting people.

I liked my classes, too. It didn't take me that long to figure out that basically, college is college, wherever. Sometimes on weekends, when I didn't want to see anyone I knew, I'd head downtown to study in the library at Amherst College—the Shangri-la of competitive colleges. Walking across campus, I'd think, *Why don't I go here?* Inside, the students weren't so unlike the ones back at U Mass, whether they were studying, napping or procrastinating. I realized that trading U Mass for any other school would be a pretty shallow move: I'd be deserting my friends and my classes so I could have some Oriental rugs and hi-pro name on my T-shirts, diploma and résumé.

Now I only occasionally wonder if going to some fancy-pants school would have made a difference in my life. My one friend from Amherst calls me every so often—collect—to beweep her unsatisfying stints as a waitress or a receptionist at a company whose name she can't pronounce. She tends to say, "God, I should have just gone to U Mass." And then, "The real world is so unfair."

Welcome to it, I think.

Rory Evans

Walt was starting to think he should have
chosen a smaller college.

If the Dream Is Big Enough,
the Facts Don't Count

I used to watch her from my kitchen window and laugh. She seemed so small as she muscled her way through the crowd of boys on the playground. The school was across the street from our home, and I often stood at my window, hands buried in dishwater or cookie dough, watching the kids as they played during recess. A sea of children, and yet to me, she stood out from them all.

I remember the first day I saw her playing basketball. I watched in wonder as she ran circles around the other kids. She managed to shoot jump-shots just over their heads and into the net. The boys always tried to stop her, but no one could.

I began to notice her at other times, on that same black-top, basketball in hand, playing alone. She practiced dribbling and shooting over and over again, sometimes until dark. One day I asked her why she practiced so much. As she turned her head, her dark ponytail whipped quickly around, and she looked directly into my eyes. Without hesitating, she said, "I want to go to college. My dad wasn't able to go to college, and he has talked to me about going for as long as I can remember. The only way

I can go is if I get a scholarship. I like basketball. I decided that if I were good enough, I would get a scholarship. I am going to play college basketball. I want to be the best. My daddy told me if the dream is big enough, the facts don't count." Then she smiled and ran toward the court to recap the routine I had seen over and over again.

Well, I had to give it to her—she was determined. I watched her through those junior high years and into high school. Every week, she led her varsity team to victory. It was always a thrill to watch her play.

One day in her senior year, I saw her sitting in the grass, head cradled in her arms. I walked across the street and sat down beside her. Quietly I asked what was wrong.

"Oh, nothing," came a soft reply. "I am just too short." The coach had told her that at five-feet, five-inches tall, she would probably never get to play for a top-ranked team—much less be offered a scholarship—so she should stop dreaming about college.

She was heartbroken, and I felt my own throat tighten as I sensed her disappointment. I asked her if she had talked to her dad about it yet.

She lifted her head from her hands and told me that her father said those coaches were wrong. They just did not understand the power of a dream. He told her that if she really wanted to play for a good college, if she truly wanted a scholarship, that nothing could stop her except one thing—her own attitude. He told her again, "If the dream is big enough, the facts don't count."

The next year, as she and her team went to the Northern California Championship game, she was seen by a college recruiter who was there to watch the opposing team. She was indeed offered a scholarship, a full ride, to an NCAA Division I women's basketball team. She accepted. She was going to get the college education that she had dreamed of and worked toward for all those years. And that little girl had more playing time as a freshman and sophomore than any other woman in the history of that university.

Late one night, during her junior year of college, her father called her. "I'm sick, Honey. I have cancer. No, don't quit school and come home. Everything will be okay. I love you."

He died six weeks later—her hero, her dad. She did leave school those last few days to support her mother and care for her father. Late one night, during the final hours before his death, he called for her in the darkness.

As she came to his side, he reached for her hand and struggled to speak. "Rachel, keep dreaming. Don't let your dream die with me. Promise me," he pleaded. "Promise me."

In those last few precious moments together, she replied, "I promise, Daddy."

Those years to follow were hard on her. She was torn between school and her family, knowing her mother was left alone with a new baby and three other children to raise. The grief she felt over the loss of her father was always there, hidden in that place she kept inside, waiting to raise its head at some unsuspecting moment and drop her again to her knees.

Everything seemed harder. She struggled daily with fear, doubt and frustration. A severe learning disability had forced her to go to school year-round for three years just to keep up with requirements. The testing facility on campus couldn't believe she had made it through even one semester. Every time she wanted to quit, she remembered her father's words: "Rachel, keep dreaming. Don't let your dream die. If the dream is big enough, you can do anything! I believe in you." And of course, she remembered the promise she made to him.

My daughter kept her promise and completed her degree. It took her six years, but she did not give up. She can still be found sometimes as the sun sets, bouncing a basketball. And often I hear her tell others, "If the dream is big enough, the facts don't count."

Cynthia Stewart-Copier

Hani

The difference between the impossible and the possible lies in a person's determination.

Tommy Lasorda

The day I met Hani Irmawati, she was a shy, seventeen-year-old girl standing alone in the parking lot of the international school in Indonesia, where I teach English. The school is expensive and does not permit Indonesian students to enroll. She walked up to me and asked if I could help her improve her English. I could tell it took immense courage for the young Indonesian girl in worn clothing to approach me and ask for my help.

"Why do you want to improve your English?" I asked her, fully expecting her to talk about finding a job in a local hotel.

"I want to go to an American university," she said with quiet confidence. Her idealistic dream made me want to cry.

I agreed to work with her after school each day on a volunteer basis. For the next several months, Hani woke each morning at five and caught the city bus to her public high school. During the one-hour ride, she studied for her regular classes and prepared the English lessons I had given her the day before. At four o'clock in the afternoon, she arrived at my classroom, exhausted but ready to work. With each passing day, as Hani struggled with college-level English, I grew more fond of her. She worked harder than most of my wealthy expatriate students.

Hani lived in a two-room house with her parents and two brothers. Her father was a building custodian and her mother was a maid. When I went to their neighborhood to meet them, I learned that their combined yearly income was 750 U.S. dollars. It wasn't enough to meet the expenses of even one month in an American university. Hani's enthusiasm was increasing with her language ability, but I was becoming more and more discouraged.

One morning in December 1998, I received the announcement of a scholarship opportunity for a major American university. I excitedly tore open the envelope and studied the requirements, but it wasn't long before I dropped the form in despair. There was just no way, I thought, for Hani to meet these qualifications. She had never led a club or an organization, because in her school these things simply did not exist. She had no guidance counselor and no impressive standardized test scores, because there were no such tests for her to take.

She did, however, have more determination than any student I'd ever seen. When Hani came into the classroom that day, I told her of the scholarship. I also told her that I believed there was no way for her to apply. I encouraged her to be, as I put it, "realistic" about her future and not to plan so strongly on coming to America. Even after my somber lecture, Hani remained steadfast.

"Will you send in my name?" she asked.

I didn't have the heart to turn her down. I completed the application, filling in each blank with the painful truth about her academic life, but also with my praise of her courage and her perseverance. I sealed up the envelope and told Hani her chances for acceptance ranged somewhere between slim and none.

In the weeks that followed, Hani increased her study of English, and I arranged for her to take the Test of English Fluency in Jakarta. The entire computerized test would be an enormous challenge for someone who had never before touched a computer. For two weeks, we studied computer parts and how they worked. Then, just before Hani went to Jakarta, she received a letter from the scholarship association. *What a cruel time for the rejection to arrive,* I thought. Trying to prepare her for disappointment, I opened the letter and began to read it to her. She had been accepted.

I leaped about the room ecstatically, shocked. Hani stood by, smiling quietly, but almost certainly bewildered by my surprise. The image of her face in that moment came back to me time and time again in the following week. I finally realized that it was I who had learned something Hani had known from the beginning: It is not intelligence alone that brings success, but also the drive to succeed, the commitment to work hard and the courage to believe in yourself.

Jamie Winship

The college I picked out costs $22,000 a year—
that's only 6¢ per minute.

Inspiration Can Be Anywhere

No one in Hannah Moore's family encouraged her to go to medical school. Her mother was a kind, loving woman, but she spent most of her time changing diapers, cooking and cleaning the two-bedroom New York City apartment where she was raising Hannah and her three siblings. Hannah's father loved her, too, but his way of showing it was by joking and telling stories about the days when he was in the circus, although everyone knew that he never had been. He worked for the city, fixing signs when they were vandalized or run over by reckless drivers. Not an educated man himself, Hannah's father thought that his kids would grow up, finish high school and find jobs as laborers, just as he had done.

Hannah didn't resent her father's lack of higher education or her mother's life as a homemaker. But she told her mother that she wanted to become a physician. Her mom said, "Honey, you know that we don't have the money to send you to medical school. You need a more practical goal like becoming a teacher or a nurse."

To twelve-year-old Hannah, this made no sense at all. She knew that if she went to college, her parents couldn't lend a dime to the endeavor regardless of what she chose to do. She didn't say that to her mom, though. She also didn't say, "C'mon, Mom, this is the 1970s. Women can do whatever they want to do, and I want to be a doctor." Hannah simply withdrew and kept her dream inside. She never mentioned it to her mother again.

She did mention it to her father, though. Two years later, as they walked home alone from the ice-cream parlor where he'd regaled her with stories about his triple somersault between flying trapezes, she said, "I'm going to go to medical school to become a doctor, Daddy."

He chuckled. "You don't want to do that, Tiger. You know my cousin, Ronnie, the nurse's assistant in Brooklyn?"

"Yeah . . ."

"Well, she complains about working in the hospital all the time. Every time I talk to her, she tells me about how the doctors ain't got no respect for the nurses and how awful it is to see drunks in the emergency room. Why don't you become an animal doctor instead? I bet animals ain't so hard to deal with."

An animal doctor? Hannah thought. *Well, I do like animals . . . but I want to be a medical missionary and help sick children in India.* She was just about to say this as she and her dad entered their apartment building, but he was already going up the steps four at a time, telling her that he used to climb the steps to the trapeze the same way. She sighed. Maybe her parents were right. Maybe medical school was an impossible dream for her or anyone in her family.

No, neither of Hannah's parents encouraged her to go to medical school. But someone did. Dr. Hannah Moore likes to tell the story about that person to her favorite patients, especially those who are just about to go off to college and those who ask her about becoming a doctor.

Mrs. Haverill was a peculiar lady. At least that's how Mrs. Moore and the other neighborhood mothers described her. All day she sang near the open window facing the street, crooning love songs to her parrot. The women frowned as they heard Mrs. Haverill's voice singing off-key. But it wasn't like the heavy metal music that the young couple on the first floor played, so how could they complain? As for Hannah, she liked Mrs. Haverill's singing. In fact, it somehow drew her to Mrs. Haverill's door. What else was in the apartment with her? Would she let Hannah see that beautiful red and blue bird up close? Curious and compelled, Hannah thought of a reason to introduce herself.

She climbed the stairs to Mrs. Haverill's landing and bravely knocked on the door. A heavyset woman about fifty years old, with her jet-black hair pulled into a bun on her head, answered the door. Her bright purple eye shadow and scarlet lipstick would have looked ridiculous on Hannah's mother, but on this woman it seemed fitting.

"Mrs. Haverill," Hannah began, "I've noticed that you have a hard time getting up and down the stairs on icy days. Would you like me to go to the grocery store for you sometimes?"

"Oh, dear child, that would be wonderful!"

Hannah's neighbor invited her in for hot chocolate after the first trip to the store. Her apartment was just as peculiar as she was, full of vines, potted trees and even more birds than the one she always sang to at the window. Hannah was fourteen at the time, and this strange place became a welcome respite from her own apartment, the kind of place every teenager needs. As she sipped the hot chocolate and looked at a cockatiel on a perch, she said, "My dad thinks that I should become a vet."

"Ah, yes, an animal doctor," Mrs. Haverill said in her singsong voice. "And what do you think?"

"I want to be a doctor for kids in India and work with Mother Teresa."

"Ah, yes, a medical missionary!" exclaimed the woman, with even more enthusiasm. "A medical missionary indeed.

Ah, yes, I hardly know you, dear child, but I can see that in you. I have a cousin who was a doctor in Africa during the 1960s. Now she runs a mobile doctor's office on the streets of the city. Ah, yes, Hannah, can you stay a while for me to tell you about her?"

That afternoon began a friendship with many visits during which a fifty-something woman told true stories to a fourteen-year-old who longed to hear them. Hannah had been raised on storytelling, but this time it was different. This time the stories were true. Hannah almost fell out of her seat when Mrs. Haverill began by saying, "Now, when we were growing up together in the Bronx, Shirley and I dreamed of running away with the circus as many children do. When she first told me that she was going to be a doctor, I thought it was just another silly dream. We were from the poorest family on the street. All of our neighbors owned the surrounding stores, but we had nothing but a few threadbare clothes. . . ."

She showed Hannah photos of her cousin donning the black graduation gown of a new doctor, as well as snapshots of her cousin in Africa. When she knew that Hannah was sincerely interested, she introduced her to Shirley, who took her to lunch at an uptown diner one afternoon in March.

When Hannah recalls the appointment with the quiet woman about whom she had learned so much, she remembers feeling unusually excited and finally encouraged.

"My mom says it costs too much to go to medical school," she said to Shirley.

The woman's voice was so soft that it was hard to believe she was Mrs. Haverill's cousin. "Are your grades good?"

"All As," Hannah answered.

"Then if it's meant to be, you'll find a way."

Hannah Moore, M.D., received a full scholarship to

Columbia. She remembers a sunny graduation day in May as one of the happiest days of her life. She recalls her first day of travel in India with similar joy. Only the births of her children were more exciting.

She returned from India with her husband just before her first child was born. "We'll all go back again when they are older," she says. Now she enjoys working as an infectious-disease specialist in a city hospital, watching her kids grow and letting them get to know their grandparents—as well as Mrs. Haverill, who still sings to her parrot near an open street-front window and offers hope when it's needed.

Cerie L. Couture

A Proposal to Myself

I am writing this the day before I know my fate—the day before I know the answer to what will happen in my life. I am writing this with my mind set that I will carry on and not let life pass me by. I am determined that I will see the world in every aspect that may be possible for me. I am sure that I will become something, even if the envelope that carries my life inside it gives me bad news.

I will not listen to those who insist that a university degree is the only way you will find a means of living these days. I will ignore those who tell me that I am a dreamer without a dream. I will tell myself that although I may not be accepted to college, I have seen the northern lights curtain themselves in front of me. I have tasted the wine in Paris and swum in the Atlantic and Pacific Oceans. I have been to an Irish pub, and I have watched the sun rise from the Roman Forum. I have climbed the Swiss Alps and counted the stars in the sky until I could see no more.

I have experienced what it is like to live, and I will tell myself that even if that envelope is small and exudes rejection, the person that they have rejected will carry on and go on to see more mountains and swim in more waters and keep on counting the stars, because some-where it is written that I must continue to live my life the way I know how to.

The envelope that will reach my mailbox tomorrow will bring an answer that I am ready to bear with courage and self-respect. I will not cry, unless they be tears of joy for bidding good-bye to my childhood and welcoming in a new life—one that is mysterious and unknown. One that will teach me to grow and understand why things are the way they are. One that will filter out all my regrets and let my self-worth multiply.

I will be strong in my battle and not let little things bring me down. I will tell myself that it is okay to be scatterbrained once in a while and that sometimes the kindness you show will balance out your faults. I will know that I am a good person and that being smart doesn't necessarily mean that you are accepted into col-lege. I know who I am and there are brain surgeons who would be challenged sorting through my multi-faceted psyche.

I am independent by nature and a proud woman. I accept who I am. And whether or not I am accepted into college, I will be true to myself and to others around me. I will learn to carry on with every good-bye I say at school this week. I will remember my friends and acquaintances and idols, and I will wish them the best of luck in life.

The envelope that has yet to reach my house will not be a letter, but rather a decision that I will make with my life. I am confused, as are most people my age around this time, but I will not look back. I will only look toward tomorrow and greet each day, wherever I am, with a smile.

Sarah Lockyer

2

TRANSITION

Out of respect for things that I was never destined to do, I have learned that my strengths are a result of my weaknesses, my success is due to my failures and my style is directly related to my limitations.

Billy Joel

Good-Bye, Mr. Blib

Mr. Blib is graduating from high school next week.

Mr. Blib is my boy. The school thinks he's ready to go away to college. He and the other members of his class also think they're ready to leave home.

But I'm here to say he's not the least bit ready.

I have taught my boy many things in eighteen years. He knows to put the knife on the right, blade in. He knows I will eventually find out what long-distance phone calls he's made because they get listed on the bill. He knows not to lie.

But as the weeks tick by before he leaves for college, it's the things I haven't yet taught him that plague me.

I don't think, for example, that he fully understands about checking accounts. I think he believes there's a check heaven, and that no one will ever be the wiser if he overdraws his account.

I'm afraid he won't keep track of the oil in his car or make sure there's air in the spare.

He still doesn't know how to line up his pant seams properly on the rare occasions that he hangs them up.

He has no instinct for shopping. When he runs out of shaving cream at school, I'm not sure it will occur to him to go buy more. Instead, I think he'll call me collect and ask me to put it on the list.

He still puts metal in the microwave once in a while, and he's never in his life managed to unwad a pair of socks before putting them in the hamper.

I also haven't taught him about the motor vehicle department. How can he possibly go away to college when he doesn't even know enough to fill out the correct forms before standing in line?

He's just not ready. No way.

On the other hand, I'm ready for him to leave. Jeez, I doubt I'll hardly miss him once he's gone.

I'm sure not going to miss the fact that he uses up all the hot water in the house. I haven't had a hot shower since he was five and started taking charge of his own hygiene.

I'm sure not going to miss his crisis-management style of living, either. Everything is an emergency in that boy's life, whether it's a missing tape cassette or hunger.

I won't miss his counsel about the mistakes I make raising his younger brother. In fact, he still dwells on the mistake I made in *having* his younger brother, and I'm tired of hearing it.

I won't miss his stubbornness, either. Once, when he was four years old, we made a deal—he would stop sucking his thumb and I would stop smoking. He quit sucking his thumb on the spot and never put it in his mouth again. I still smoke.

What kind of person is that to have around the house? Who would miss such a stubborn, strong-willed boy? He's like this about everything.

And noisy! I'm sure not going to miss how noisy he is. He's always laughing too loud. He's so ready to see the humor in something, he even laughs when I tell a story that makes him look the fool.

Like the Mr. Blib story. I call him Mr. Blib because he once told me he was blib.

"You know Mom, I'm pretty blib," he told me.

"Blib?" I said. "What's blib?"

"You know—good with words," he said glibly.

Now who could miss such a blib boy? A boy who laughs at himself when I tell this story?

I'm sure not going to miss talking to him at the dinner table or having a late-night snack with him when he comes home from a date. And skiing with him—why would I miss that? He goes too fast, anyhow.

And I sure won't miss him relying on me for advice. What's the big deal? Who cares if he starts making all his own decisions and doesn't need me anymore?

Look, I'm ready for this, no problem.

It's just him. He's the one I'm worried about.

Beth Mullally

A Dad Says Good-Bye

I watched her and her mother decorate her college dormitory room. Everything in place, organized and arranged, just so. Attractively designed bulletin board with carefully selected, and precisely cut, colored paper. Pictures and remembrances throughout of her dearest friends. Drawers and boxes under the bed. Her room nicely accommodates not only her clothes, accessories and bric-a-brac, but her roommate's as well. I closely monitor that which I would have, in the past, ignored, knowing that this time is different. As her half of the room takes on her essence, I begin to accept that her room at home is no longer hers. It is now ours. Our room for her when she visits.

I find myself thinking of when I held her in the cradle of my arm, in the chair alongside my wife's hospital bed. One day old. So small, so beautiful, so perfect, so totally reliant on her new, untested parents. All manner of thoughts went through my mind as I examined her every feature for what seemed to be an eternity. Time marches relentlessly.

She looks up now, catching me staring at her, causing her to say to her mother, "Mom, Dad's looking at me funny."

The last few days, I touch her arm, her face—any thing—knowing that when my wife and I return home, she will not be with us and there will be nothing to touch. I have so much to say, but no words with which to say it.

My life changed from the day I drove this child home from the hospital. I saw myself differently that day, and it has led to a lot of places that I would never have found on my own.

She says, "It'll be all right, Dad. I'll be home from school soon." I tell her she will have a great year, but I say little else. I am afraid somehow to speak, afraid I'll say something too small for what I'm feeling, and so I only hold on to our good-bye hug a little longer, a little tighter.

I gaze into her eyes and turn to go. My wife's eyes follow her as she leaves us. Mine do not. Maybe if I don't look, I can imagine that she really hasn't gone. I know that what she is embarking upon is exciting and wonderful. I remember what the world looked like to me when everything was new.

As I walk to the car with my wife at my side, my eyes are wet, my heart is sore, and I realize that my life is changing forever.

Joseph Danziger

College Talk

It seemed to come on like the flu. Suddenly, out of nowhere, everyone was talking about college. Lunchtime discussions changed from who's dating whom into who's going to what college and who did or did not get accepted. And just like the flu leaves its victims feeling awful and helpless, such was the case for this new fascinating subject and me.

I don't clearly remember the actual conversations. I do, however, remember why I wasn't interested in all this "college talk." We didn't have enough money for me to go to a real college. I would begin my college years at a junior college. This was the final word and I had accepted it. I didn't even mind terribly. I just wished everyone would stop talking about this university and that Ivy League school.

The truth is, I was jealous. I had worked so hard to get good grades in school and for what? Each time I found out someone else I knew had just been accepted to the college of their dreams I would turn a deeper shade of green. I didn't like feeling this way, but I couldn't help it. It felt like they were going to jump ahead of me. They were going to have the big life experiences that turn a teenager into an adult and I was going to get left behind.

My boyfriend was very sweet and barely mentioned it every time an envelope arrived for him with a "Congratulations, you've been accepted to yet another college of your choice!" I knew about them only because his parents lacked the sensitivity with which he was so blessed. He always shrugged it off and would tell me, "You would have had the same response. Watch, you'll get a full scholarship to the college of your choice in two years and you can laugh at us all for foolishly killing ourselves to arrive at the same place." He had a point. I just thought it was awfully sweet of him to make sure I saw it this way.

My friends and I kept in touch those first few months and, more often than not, I was the one offering words of support and understanding. They spoke of roommates from hell, classes they couldn't get into, and the ones they did being so big they couldn't even see their professor. Not only could I see mine, but one of my favorites invited us to his house on a lake. We would go there for class and stay hours afterwards talking and sharing our theories on human behavior. It was because of this class that I decided to major in psychology.

Needless to say, my tortured thoughts of being left behind while they went out and gathered life experiences in huge doses changed to thoughts of counting my blessings. I was getting a fine serving of life experience. I was letting go of friends and my first true love. I was moving into a humble abode that for the first time in my life I could call my own and I was taking a full load of classes by choice, not requirement.

As time passed and I grew more and more comfortable with my circumstances, I was also able to understand something I hadn't when I was angry and envious. Real life will be filled with moments of friends making more or loved ones being promoted first. When these things happen, I know I will be prepared. I have already had a taste of this experience and I passed the test quite nicely.

Kimberly Kirberger

The "No Hug" Rule

The first day of kindergarten
He hurried to the door
Shrugging off his mother's hugs
He didn't need them anymore
For he was all grown up now
Too big for all that stuff
Instead he waved a quick good-bye
Hoping that would be enough

When he came home from school that day
She asked what he had done
He handed her a paper
With a big round yellow sun
A picture quite imperfect
For he'd messed up here and there
But she didn't seem to notice
Or she didn't seem to care

The first day of junior high
He hurried to the door
Running from his mother's hugs
He didn't want them anymore

He ignored her calling out to him
As he hurried down the street
Near the intersection
Where his friends had planned to meet
He hoped that she would understand
Why he had to walk to school
Riding with his mother
Just wouldn't have been cool

And when he came home from school
She asked what he had done
He handed her some papers
With Xs marked on more than one
The teacher clearly pointing out
The wrong answers here and there
But his mother didn't seem to notice
Or she didn't seem to care

The first day of senior high
He hurried out the door
Jumped into the driver's seat
Of his jacked-up shiny Ford
He left without his breakfast
He left without a word
But he turned and looked back
Before pulling from the curb
He saw her waving frantically
As he drove away
He tapped his horn just once
To brighten up her day
He saw a smile cross her face
And then he drove from sight
Onward to a different world
A new exciting life

And at his graduation
As tears shone in her eyes
He knew the time had come
To bid his mom good-bye
For he was off to college
Off to better days
No more rules to abide
Alone to find his way

Suitcases filled the trunk
Of his dirty beat-up Ford
He couldn't wait to get to school
To check out his room and dorm
She opened up his car door
Closed it when he got in
Then smiled proudly at her son
As tears dropped from her chin
She reached through the open window
Wished him luck in school
And then she pulled him close to her
And broke the "no hug" rule
He felt the freedom greet him
As he pulled out on the interstate
At last his life was his alone
He anticipated fate

College life was more challenging
Than he ever could have hoped
There was no time to respond to letters
His mother often wrote
He was a grown adult now
Too old for all that stuff
His visits during holidays
Would have to be enough
Besides, midterms were quickly coming

The pressure was immense
He studied late into the night
His need to pass intense
He wondered how he'd manage
How he'd ever cope
What if he failed his tests?
Would there be no hope?

As if he had a calling
He headed down the interstate
Driving at full speed
The hour getting late
He pulled up to the curb
Where once he used to roam
And went through the open door
Of his mother's home
She was sitting at the table
With a drawing in a frame
Memories from the past
That brought both joy and pain
She didn't need to ask
Why he was home from school
Because she knew the answer
When he broke the "no hug" rule
His arms around her tightly
Peering at the drawing he had done
Lots of trees, imperfect branches
And a big round yellow sun
She smiled a knowing smile
And then she spoke aloud
"Son you always did
And you always will make me very proud
For look how far you've traveled
From that little boy so brave
Heading off to kindergarten

Your hand up in a wave
And through the years you've made mistakes
But son I've made them, too
Being perfect is not an option in life
Simply do the best you can do
And don't expect more than that
For life is supposed to be fun
You've only got one to live
Do what is best for you son"

Sitting in his dorm room
When the pressure seems too much
And all that he is striving for
Seems completely out of touch
He peers at the drawing
Of a big round yellow sun
And then he is reminded
Of just how far he's come
From childhood to manhood
Fighting back many a fear
Through trials and tribulations
Holding back many a tear
Knowing that being successful
Isn't passing every test
And the only way to falter in life
Is by failing to do his best
And the biggest lesson he's learned
One he did not learn in school . . .
That it's okay, for even a man
To break the "no hug" rule

Cheryl Costello-Forshey

Shoes in the Shower

You've never done this before. You can't even come up with some neat comparison to a past experience to make you feel less awkward. It doesn't help that everyone else is doing it, since it's because of them that you have to do it in the first place. Suddenly you have to accept this totally backward behavior as if it were logical, from now on, no end in sight.

In college you wear shoes in the shower. You are halfway across the country, living by yourself for probably the first time. Your childhood seems like it's over. You are surrounded by people you don't know, from places you've never been, who probably *all* have athlete's foot. Your dorm room is supposed to be the same one you saw on your college tour, but *you* know it's smaller, colder and uglier than the one you saw when your mom was with you. You walk in and are standing in front of a girl you've never met, who you will have to live with all year. She is dressed differently from you and is from a state you've never visited. You probably have nothing in common. No amount of protective footwear is too drastic under these circumstances.

The first few days are like a dream. The shower continues to be the testing ground for your ability to adapt to these conditions. You are sure that everyone but you has figured out how to shave her legs in these small cubicles. You glance wistfully at the people in the hall, wondering who could possibly fill in for the best friend you left at home, in whose bathroom you could always go barefoot.

You cry yourself to sleep a couple of times and find yourself counting the days until Thanksgiving. What were you thinking? The state college thirty minutes away would have been just fine, probably much safer. You call home and tell your parents how homesick you are. Sure, you went to that party Saturday night, which was okay, but surely they understand that that's nothing compared to your misery. Your parents say "Give it a chance" so often that you become convinced that they are putting the phone down next to the family parrot and walking away.

But after a while, the Shoeless Night happens. It comes to everybody, sooner or later. Perhaps for you it is a midnight McDonald's run with some girls on your floor and a post-McNugget conversation, way into the night. Your fear of various foot diseases begins to fade somewhat. You might actually like some of the girls.

You might still cry yourself to sleep that night, but something's changed. For a few hours, you got to remove the mythical shoes from the feet of your soul. Because the important thing about The Night is that it is followed by Other Nights. The night of party hopping is preceded by a two-hour primping session with the same girls, before piling far too many of you into one car. The night of stealing other halls' furniture together allows you to let them see you in the morning after an "I'm too tired to wash my face" night.

Eventually, when you need to cry (because you still might, for a while), you find yourself walking down the hall to someone else's room instead of getting on the phone to your parents. When you do call them, all you can talk about is that girl down the hall who understands everything you say and listens so well. Your parents are thrilled and begin teaching the parrot to say, "That's great, Honey!"

One night while standing at a party, you turn to your friend and say, "Are you ready to go home?" Then you realize you're referring to your dorm, that place that seemed so cold and ugly the first week. Well, they must have turned the heat up, or repainted or something. You still wear shoes in the shower, but you and your friends know it's just because of those people on the next floor.

You can't be too careful.

Lia Gay and Rebecca Hart

Reprinted by permission of Joan Wiberg.

Deck the Halls

Christmas at my house was always a major event. My mom insisted that we play Christmas music and only Christmas music—all the time and starting two weeks before the "big day." We'd bake Santa-shaped cookies and give them to our friends and neighbors. Every year, my sister and I decorated the house with porcelain figurines that had been in the family for eons. Each year we'd track down the perfect tree at the local "U-Cut" Christmas-tree farm.

Of course, I'll admit that there were times when the mere thought of spending yet another Saturday listening to Bing and Mom crooning "White Christmas" made me want to stuff a stocking down any songster's merry little throat. And the prospect of my annual fight with my sister over the ideal shape of a Douglas fir was about as appealing as, say, running into Steve Urkel under the mistletoe.

Then I went to college. Sure, there was no curfew, no obligatory family dinners; but when December rolled around, there was also no baking, decorating or music. Just the exam panic and 3:00 A.M. diet soda binges. By December 13, with ten more anxiety-filled days to go before my last final, I was totally depressed and desperately homesick. I decided to take action.

"This stinks," I declared to my equally stressed-out roommate. "Put down your highlighter pen. I need a little Christmas, right this very minute. Carols at the window, candles on the spinet!" It was bad. I was leaking sappy Christmas tunes from home, and I knew I had to do something about it—quick! Luckily, my roommate was feeling the same way. We both tossed our books aside and prepared to outdo Macy's with our version of Christmas cheer.

In a Martha Stewart-like frenzy, we fashioned red and green construction paper into signs that read "MERRY XMAS" and taped them to our walls. Then we cut snowflake wannabes from typing paper and made our own winter wonderland. We microwaved popcorn, strung some of it, ate most of it, and then hung the strings artfully around the room.

Finally, we stepped back to examine our work. Something was missing. Andy Williams singing "Joy to the World"? Antler headbands? No, duh—lights! So we grabbed a cab to the nearest discount store and bought miles of multicolored bulbs.

Back in our room, we went through three rolls of duct tape trying to get the look we so desperately craved. Around the door, veering erratically across the ceiling and up the window, we fashioned an Impressionistic Christmas-tree shape. When we plugged the lights in, it was a sight to behold. I popped a Christmas tape that my mom had sent me into the tape deck, and the moment was complete.

To further foster the feeling of Christmas, I insisted that the group of girls on my floor do a secret Santa gift exchange. Everybody drew a name out of a hat and bought that person a gift. Then we all got together, opened our presents and tried to guess who our secret Santa was. Sitting there in a sea of shower gels, posters of cute guys and Lifesaver's Sweet Storybooks, I started choking up. It was at that moment I realized how special, wonderful and beautiful my mom had made this holiday for all of us in our family. It was a part of me, even if I was locked in a dorm with a bunch of girls cramming for exams, I had to have it.

Sure, it was Christmas college-style with Rice Krispy treats instead of rice pudding, and Pearl Jam instead of the Hallelujah Chorus; but we were stuck at school, and we got to create our own traditions. I'm a senior now, and we still do the secret Santa thing. My roommate and I have also lugged boxes of ornaments and hauled nasty-looking fake Christmas trees around from dorms to two apartments, but as long as I live, I will never forget our first heartfelt, makeshift college Christmas.

Melanie Fester

Yes, Dad, I suppose I could've been more specific
when I asked you to mail me a big check.

Reprinted by permission of David M. Cooney.

The Times I Called Home from College

- When I got off the plane
- When I met my roommate
- When I had to select a long-distance phone company
- When I wanted my stereo sent to me
- When I fought with my roommate
- When I needed money
- When I needed to know how to make mashed potatoes
- When I put liquid dish soap in the dishwasher
- When I wanted to know how to get soy sauce out of rayon
- When I got in a car accident
- When I failed a test
- When I met a special girl
- When I lost a special girl
- When I got lonely
- When I got a kitten
- When I got fleas
- When I didn't want to study
- When I needed money
- When they sent me a care package

- When I got a good grade
- When I got published in the school newspaper
- When it was my mom's birthday
- When it was my birthday
- When I needed help moving out of the dorms
- When I changed majors
- When I changed majors again
- When we won the big game
- When we went to war in the Gulf
- When there were riots
- When I gave up meat
- When I wanted my parents to give up meat
- When I needed money
- When I got the flu
- When my parents had an anniversary
- When Grandpa died
- When there was an earthquake
- When I met someone famous
- When I needed money
- When I got a night job
- When I needed advice
- When a friend from high school got cancer
- When I felt no one understood
- When I wanted a ticket home
- When I won an award
- When I needed a relative's address
- When I ran out of stamps
- When I wanted some homemade cookies
- When I needed money
- When I just wanted to tell them I loved them

Scott Greenberg

Learning to do your own laundry is a fundamental part of life as a college freshman.

The Long Road Home

I find myself packing again. Well, let's be completely honest, this isn't really packing—it's shoving three weeks' worth of dirty clothes into a suitcase and having my roommate sit on it so I can get it to close.

This time is different; this isn't the same nostalgic trip down memory lane as when I packed before college. This is the "night before my first trip home frantic pack." So you get the idea—my plane leaves in two hours, and no, college didn't teach me to procrastinate. I was experienced in that art long before I stepped onto my college campus.

So now that I'm packed, I have a minute to examine my emotions about my first trip home. I'm excited. My best friend, Matt, picks me up, groggy, for our 4:00 A.M. drive. My expectations are that I am going home to what I left: my parents, home-cooked meals, friends with whom I shared distinctive bonds and my long-distance boyfriend, whom I have been dying to see. I am happy at college, but a trip home, to my family and friends, sounds like just the thing I need to prepare me for the prefinals crunch.

I think I will catch up on the missed hours of sleep on the plane. Instead, I look around and realize that most of the exhausted passengers are students just like me. Below us, in the cargo bin, sits a year's worth of dirty laundry at least.

I miss my connecting flight, so I am later than expected. I step off the plane to find my mom frantic, thinking I had been "abducted" on the trip home. I look at her puzzled. I guess in a mother's eyes there is no logical explanation for being late, such as the obvious flight trouble. I assure her that I am fine and that I don't need to fly as an "unaccompanied minor" on the way back.

A few hours later, I'm back at the airport, waiting for my boyfriend's arrival home. He steps off the plane with the same groggy but excited look I wore hours before. We drive over to see my dad, who seems calmer than my mother had been. I ask to see my room, expecting to find my shrine, my old pompoms, prom pictures, candid photos of friends and dolls scattered about. To my surprise, everything is gone; there's not even a trace I had ever lived in the room. I'm starting to wonder if I really had been abducted on the way home. It's as if the second I became a "college" student, I had ceased to exist.

I start to wonder what else had changed since I'd been gone. My parents are in an awkward transition, wondering how to treat me now. They wrestle with whether to treat me—still their daughter—as one of them, an adult, or as the child they feel they sent away months earlier.

I run into two of my best friends from high school; we stare blankly at each other. We ask the simple questions and give simple, abrupt answers. It's as if we have nothing to say to each other. I wonder how things have changed so much in such a small amount of time. We used to laugh and promise that no matter how far away we were, our love for each other would never change. Their interests don't interest me anymore, and I find myself unable to relate my life to theirs.

I had been so excited to come home, but now I just look at it all and wonder: *Is it me?*

Why hadn't the world stood still here while I was gone? My room isn't the same, my friends and I don't share the same bond, and my parents don't know how to treat me—or who I am, for that matter.

I get back to school feeling half-fulfilled, but not disappointed. I sit up in my bed in my dorm room, surrounded by my pictures, dolls and mementos. As I wonder what has happened, I realize that I can't expect the world to stand still and move forward at the same time. I can't change and expect that things at home will stay the same. I have to find comfort in what has changed and what is new; keep the memories, but live in the present.

A few weeks later, I'm packing again, this time for winter break. My mom meets me at the curb. I have come home accepting the changes, not only in my surroundings, but most of all in me.

Lia Gay

Reprinted by permission of Joan Wiberg.

Breakdown of Family Traced to Psych. 1 Student

It's what you learn after you know it all that counts.

John Wooden

There is no joy quite like a visit from your college kid after he's taken half a semester of Psychology 1.

Nosirree.

Suddenly you're living with Little Freud, and he's got your number. With all this education, he now knows that a) your habit of washing the dishes after each meal is obsessive-compulsive, b) you smoke because you're orally fixated, and c) you're making terrible mistakes raising his younger brother.

No behavior escapes Little Freud's scrutiny. The simplest conversations take on profound and incomprehensible meaning.

Getting Little Freud out of bed in the morning, for example, suddenly becomes a control issue:

"It's past noon," says the simple-minded mother. "Why don't you get up?"

"Mom," says Little Freud in a voice fraught with meaningful implication, "you're obsessing. You shouldn't disempower me this way. Why allow my behavior to affect your own sense of self? Besides, I have to stay in bed for a while to experience the consciousness of my being when my being is in nothingness."

"That's easy for you to say," says the simple-minded mother. "But I say you're sleeping. Now get up and help rake the leaves."

"Classic transference," says Little Freud in such a way that the simple-minded mother can only conclude she must have a psychic ailment as repulsive as fungus.

Little Freud also knows now that nothing is as simple as it might seem. Calling him to dinner can set off an analysis of your childhood:

"Dinner's ready," says Simple Mind.

"Don't you think it's time you stopped taking your Oedipal rage out on me?" asks Little Freud. "Just because you could never lure your father away from your mother is no reason to resent me."

"What are you talking about?" asks Simple Mind. "I said it's time to eat. What does that have to do with Oedipus?"

"In your unconscious, you associate food with pre-Oedipal gratification, which sets off a chain of associative thoughts leading straight to your rage, which you cannot acknowledge and, therefore, you transfer your hostility to me."

"Be quiet and eat your dinner before it gets cold," says Simple Mind.

"Aha!" says Little Freud, triumphant. "You see? Classic regression."

Little Freud is also a skilled marriage counselor now that he's done so much studying:

"I think it's time you two confronted your feelings," Little Freud tells his parents, who are simple-mindedly enjoying a bottle of wine in front of the fireplace.

"We can't. We're playing cards," says Mr. Simple Mind. "Your mother and I have a policy against confronting our feelings and playing cards at the same time."

"Classic avoidance," declares Little Freud.

Little Freud is at his most eloquent, though, when he points out how wrong his simple-minded parents are about their method of raising kids:

"You're not parenting him properly," says Little Freud of his younger brother. "You're too permissive, probably because you're projecting your desire to be free of the shackles of your own stifled childhood."

"What are you talking about?" says the simple-minded mother, who is getting pretty tired of asking Little Freud what he's talking about.

"And he also seems to have a lot of rage," says Little Freud, plunging on. "His id has taken over, and his super-ego has collapsed. He seems to be entertaining some classic primordial fixations. In fact, I think he wants to kill me."

"He doesn't really want to kill you, dear," says Simple Mind. "I've hired him to do it for me."

"Classic projection," says Little Freud, disgustedly.

Beth Mullally

3

LESSONS FROM THE CLASSROOM

The illiterate of the future will not be the person who cannot read. It will be the person who does not know how to learn.

Alvin Toffler

Undeclared

It echoed through the hallways and out onto the quad like some ancient Gregorian chant. Everyone was asking it. It was the new catchphrase. It was the new pickup line—more popular than "What's your sign?" But I had no answer. I dreaded the question. I was *undeclared*, like some contraband being smuggled across an international border. Like an astronaut floating untethered through space, I had no purpose in life. I would rather have taken the SAT again than have to face the question, "What's your major?"

And tomorrow was the last day to declare a major. The last day! Everyone else was happily moving forward in their lives, striving toward careers in anthropology, sociology, molecular biology and the like. "Don't worry," my friends would say. "You can always major in business." Business? Not me. I was an artist. I would rather have died than majored in business. In fact, I didn't even need college. I could just go out into the world, and my great talents would be immediately recognized.

On the night before my fate was to be declared, my parents were having a dinner party for some of their friends. Sanctuary! What would my parents' friends care about majors? I could eat dinner in peace and take a break from my inner angst for a couple of hours.

I was wrong. All they could talk about was majors. They each had to share their majors with me, and each had an opinion as to what mine should be. All their advice didn't put me any closer to a major. It just confused me even more. None of our dinner guests seemed particularly suited for their chosen professions. Dr. Elkins, the dentist, had spinach in his teeth. Mrs. Jenkins, the industrial chemist, put ketchup on her veal. And Mr. Albertson, the hydro-engineer, kept knocking over his water glass.

Dinner was over, everyone left, the night was getting later, and yet I was still *undeclared.* I got out the catalog and began paging through the possibilities for the millionth time. Aeronautical engineering? I get airsickness. Chinese? I'd always wanted to go to China, but it seemed I could go there without majoring in it. Dentistry? Just then I happened to look in the mirror and notice spinach in my teeth. This was hopeless.

As college students are prone to do, I decided that if I just slept for a while and woke up really early, I would be able to manifest a major. I don't know exactly what it is in the college student's brain that thinks some magical process occurs between 2:00 A.M. and 6:00 A.M. that will suddenly make everything more clear.

It had worked for me in the past, but not this time. In fact, as college students are also prone to do, I overslept. I woke up at 10:00 A.M. I had missed my first class, Physics for Poets, and I had three hours to commit the rest of my life to something, anything. There was always business.

I left for campus hoping for a divine major-declaring inspiration between my house and the administration building that would point me in the right direction. Maybe a stranger would pass by on the street and say, "This is what you should do for the rest of your life: animal husbandry." Maybe I would see someone hard at work and become inspired to pursue the same career. I did see a troupe of Hare Krishnas who didn't seem particularly troubled about majors, but that didn't quite seem to be a career path suited to my temperament. I passed a movie theater playing *Once Is Not Enough*, and was tempted to duck inside and enjoy the film based on Jacqueline Susann's bestselling novel and starring David Janssen. I passed up the temptation. But, wait a minute! Movies. I *love* movies! I could major in movies. No, there is no major in movies. *Film, you idiot*, I thought. That's it! I was lost but now I was found. I was *declared*.

Fifteen years later, I think of all my friends who so confidently began college with their majors declared. Of those who went around snottily asking, "What's your major?" very few are working in their chosen professions. I didn't end up a filmmaker. In fact, I'm now on my fourth career—and some days, I still feel *undeclared*. It really doesn't matter what you major in, as long as you get the most out of college. Study what interests you, and enjoy learning about the world. There is plenty of time to decide what you will do with the rest of your life.

Tal Vigderson

Making the Grade

In 1951, I was eighteen and traveling with all the money I had in the world—fifty dollars. I was on a bus heading from Los Angeles to Berkeley. My dream of attending the university was coming true. I'd already paid tuition for the semester and for one month at the co-op residence. After that, I had to furnish the rest—my impoverished parents couldn't rescue me.

I'd been on my own as a live-in mother's helper since I was fifteen, leaving high school at noon to care for children till midnight. All through high school and my first year of college, I'd longed to participate in extracurricular activities, but my job made that impossible. Now that I was transferring to Berkeley, I hoped to earn a scholarship.

That first week I found a waitress job, baby-sat and washed dishes at the co-op as part of my rent. At the end of the semester, I had the B average I needed for a scholarship. All I had to do was achieve the B average next term.

It didn't occur to me to take a snap course; I'd come to the university to learn something. I believed I could excel academically and take tough subjects.

One such course was a survey of world literature. It was taught by Professor Sears Jayne, who roamed the stage of a huge auditorium, wearing a microphone while lecturing to packed rows. There was no text. Instead, we used paperbacks. Budgetwise, this made it easier since I could buy them as needed.

I was fascinated with the concepts he presented. To many students, it was just a degree requirement, but to me it was a feast of exciting ideas. My co-op friends who were also taking the course asked for my help. We formed a study group, which I led.

When I took the first exam—all essay questions—I was sure I'd done well. On the ground floor, amid tables heaped with test booklets, I picked out mine. There in red was my grade, a 77, C-plus. I was shocked. English was my best subject! To add insult to injury, I found that my study-mates had received Bs. They thanked me for my coaching.

I confronted the teaching assistant, who referred me to Professor Jayne, who listened to my impassioned arguments but remained unmoved.

I'd never questioned a teacher about a grade before—never had to. It didn't occur to me to plead my need for a scholarship; I wanted justice, not pity. I was convinced that my answers merited a higher grade.

I resolved to try harder, although I didn't know what that meant because school had always been easy for me. I'd used persistence in finding jobs or scrubbing floors, but not in pushing myself intellectually. Although I chose challenging courses, I was used to coasting toward As.

I read the paperbacks more carefully, but my efforts yielded another 77. Again, C-plus for me and Bs and As for my pals, who thanked me profusely. Again, I returned to Dr. Jayne and questioned his judgment irreverently. Again, he listened patiently, discussed the material with me, but wouldn't budge—the C-plus stood. He seemed fascinated by my ardor in discussing the course ideas, but my dreams of a scholarship and extracurricular activities were fading fast.

One more test before the final. One more chance to redeem myself. Yet another hurdle loomed. The last book we studied, T. S. Eliot's *The Wasteland,* was available only in hardback. Too expensive for my budget.

I borrowed it from the library. However, I knew I needed my own book to annotate. I couldn't afford a big library fine either. In 1951, there were no copying machines, so it seemed logical to haul out my trusty old Royal manual typewriter and start copying all 420 lines. In between waitressing, washing dishes, attending classes, baby-sitting, and tutoring the study group, I managed to pound them out.

I redoubled my efforts for this third exam. For the first time, I learned the meaning of the word "thorough." I'd never realized how hard other students struggled for what came easily to me.

My efforts did absolutely no good. Everything, down to the dreaded 77, went as before. Back I marched into Dr. Jayne's office. I dragged out my dog-eared, note-blackened texts, arguing my points as I had done before. When I came to the sheaf of papers that were my typed copy of *The Wasteland,* he asked, "What's this?"

"I had no money left to buy it, so I copied it." I didn't think this unusual. Improvising was routine for me.

Something changed in Dr. Jayne's usually jovial face. He was quiet for a long time. Then we returned to our regular lively debate on what these writers truly meant. When I left, I still had my third 77—definitely not a lucky number for me—and the humiliation of being a seminar leader, trailing far behind my ever-grateful students.

The last hurdle was the final. No matter what grade I got, it wouldn't cancel three C-pluses. I might as well kiss the scholarship good-bye. Besides, what was the use? I could cram till my eyes teared, and the result would be a crushing 77.

I skipped studying. I felt I knew the material as well as I ever would. Hadn't I reread the books many times and explained them to my buddies? Wasn't *The Wasteland* resounding in my brain? The night before the final, I treated myself to a movie.

I sauntered into the auditorium and decided that for once I'd have fun with a test. I marooned all the writers we'd studied on an island and wrote a debate in which they argued their positions. It was silly, befitting my nothing-to-lose mood. The words flowed—all that sparring with Dr. Jayne made it effortless.

A week later, I strolled down to the ground floor (ground zero for me) and unearthed my test from the heaps of exams. There, in red ink on the blue cover, was an A. I couldn't believe my eyes.

I hurried to Dr. Jayne's office. He seemed to be expecting me, although I didn't have an appointment. I launched into righteous indignation. How come I received a C-plus every time I slaved and now, when I'd written a spoof, I earned an A?

"I knew that if I gave you the As you deserved, you wouldn't continue to work as hard."

I stared at him, realizing that his analysis and strategy were correct. I had worked my head off, as I had never done before.

He rose and pulled a book from his crowded shelves. "This is for you."

It was a hardback copy of *The Wasteland*. On the flyleaf was an inscription to me. For once in my talkative life, I was speechless.

I was speechless again when my course grade arrived: A-plus. I believe it was the only A-plus given.

Next year, when I received my scholarship:

I cowrote, acted, sang and danced in an original musical comedy produced by the Associated Students. It played in the largest auditorium to standing-room-only houses.

I reviewed theater for the *Daily Cal,* the student campus newspaper.

I wrote a one-act play, among the first to debut at the new campus theater.

I acted in plays produced by the drama department.

The creative spark that had been buried under dishes, diapers and drudgery now flamed into life. I don't recall much of what I learned in those courses of long ago, but I'll never forget the fun I had writing and acting.

And I've always remembered Dr. Jayne's lesson. Know that you have untapped powers within you. That you must use them, even if you can get by without trying. That you alone must set your own standard of excellence.

Varda One

The Good, the Bad and the Emmy

"And the winner is . . ."

What a thrill to rush onstage to receive my Emmy for "Best Children's Program." The applause. The cheers. All the long hours and hard work put into writing and producing *Jim Henson's Muppet Babies* had paid off in a big way.

A lofty time like this is even more thrilling when compared to your low times. Times when you're certain a high like this isn't even possible. I'm talking crash, boom, *thud* times! Like that bottom-of-the-barrel time I had back in college . . .

Long before I was an Emmy winner, I was a drama student at San Diego State University. Every senior in the department is required to direct and produce a one-act play. It's a senior's biggest project—the crowning achievement of his or her college career. I was eager for my turn, determined to *write* and direct my own play. After all, if Woody Allen could write and direct his own material, so could I.

The drama department, however, felt differently. They had a strict rule that *no* student could direct a one-act play that he or she had written. It was a rule I disagreed with then and still disagree with today. Despite my arguments, the department heads wouldn't budge. So, clever lad that I am, I submitted a one-act play I had written under a pseudonym, George Spelvin. My clever plan worked.

My play, I mean George's play, *The Life of the Party*, was a farce. I chose my cast carefully, and we had a ball rehearsing. We were positive we had a collegiate hit on our hands. Eventually, our play was ready for its technical dress rehearsal.

The "tech-dress" took place the day before the performance and was the only opportunity the director and cast had to add sound effects, lighting, props and costumes— feats all performed by student technicians. It was the techies' first exposure to the play and my cast's first exposure to an audience, albeit a small one.

We launched into our tech-dress rehearsal with excitement and enthusiasm, and the techies performed their jobs admirably. My actors, on the other hand, were having a tough time. Somehow, with the addition of costumes and a set and under hot lights, this farce didn't play very funny. It creaked and groaned. My actors expected to hear laughs from the techies, but the laughs never came. Were the techies too busy? Didn't they have a sense of humor? My actors' confidence was shaken, and so was mine.

Afterward the head technician approached me and said, "You know the old saying: A bad dress rehearsal makes for a great opening!" I tried to smile back. This wasn't just a bad rehearsal; it felt like a ride on the Hindenburg. I put on my bravest face for my cast, gave a few notes and assured them they'd be terrific for the next day's performance. Tired, weary and skeptical, my actors retreated to their dorms.

The next day, the most anticipated day of my college career, I watched as the theater filled with students and faculty. I crossed my fingers as the lights went down and the music came up. To put the audience in the mood for a farce, I chose Carl Stalling's musical theme from *The Bugs Bunny Show*. Just hearing the music, the audience roared with laughter. I relaxed and uncrossed my fingers. What was there to worry about?

Plenty! My actors made their entrances, and, in the beginning, there was a smattering of laughter. The audience was rooting for them. They wanted to be entertained. As the show progressed, however, the laughs became fewer and fewer ... before they disappeared altogether. Soon, my actors were sweating—and it wasn't because of the hot lights. There were long stretches of inappropriate silence. Nothing was working. The play was dreadful, too painful to watch. I watched the audience instead. Watched them glance at their watches, watched them cough, roll their eyes. The second the play was over, they bolted for the nearest exit. Yes, it stank, but they behaved as if they actually required fresh air.

Once the theater cleared, directing class began. It didn't feel like a class, though; it felt more like a funeral. Classmates extended their condolences. The professor, a gruff German who was short on stature and charm, looked at me and said, "How did this shit happen?"

At that moment, I yearned for a black hole in the universe to swallow me whole. How did this happen? How did my comedy become a tragedy? I had always pictured this day, my college career peak, as bright and sunny ... not a dark and brooding thunderstorm.

I went back to my dorm and crashed. I mustered the strength to call my parents long-distance and report the awful events. I sobbed. My mother, wanting to comfort me but not sure how, said simply, "Honey, isn't it better to fail now than later in your professional career?" I hung up on her.

What career? Couldn't she see my professional dreams going up in smoke? How could she have uttered such a ridiculous statement? Leave it to a mother to think a little bandage could cure all!

Time passed. Life trudged on. And as I began to heal, I started to see the smallest, tiniest kernel of wisdom in my mother's statement. Yes, from my failure came an opportunity. An opportunity to examine my mistakes. An opportunity to study Woody Allen's films over and over again. I researched comedy in a deadly serious manner. I dedicated myself to understanding what was funny and why it was funny. Studied it like a student possessed. If only I could be given a second chance!

That chance came shortly after college. I was hired as a performer at a professional dinner theater, and after several months, I convinced the producer to let me direct a comedy I had written. This was a golden opportunity to put my newfound observations to the test. My cast and I worked diligently. The lights went up, and once again I crossed my fingers—and this time I kept them crossed. The laughs came. They continued. They built. The comedy was a hit, and my career was launched. I had learned well from my collegiate mistakes.

Today—with over 150 programs to my credit—I've experienced both successes and failures. I continue to learn from my failures but don't take them as seriously. Nor do I take my successes too seriously, either. I enjoy them, learn from them, too, and move on. What's important is that we keep improving. Keep honing our skills. Keep striving to be our best.

I urge you to do the same. Don't let the low times keep you down. Learn from them and reach for the high times. Who knows, maybe the future holds an Emmy with your name on it, too!

David Wiemers

The Thought Card

I often wonder how people survive childhood and adolescence at all, don't you? Children take so many risks and do so many crazy things that it's hard to see how they manage to get through it all. When they get to adolescence, it gets even crazier. Tossed around on seas of hormones, pushed and pulled by the winds of impulses, and drawn by the hope of hidden treasure in relationships with friends and others, adolescents can sometimes drown in all the confusion.

I must admit that I personally was still an angry adolescent in my first years of college. My anger was diffuse—the world didn't please me in almost any way. My anger was focused—my parents didn't please me at all. I chafed under my father's direction and correction.

Our finances were limited, so I chose to go to a local college and commute to classes every day. One day I had a serious fight with my father. I saw him as controlling me and wanted to break free. He saw me as rebellious and tried to reassert his authority. We both exploded in shouts. I stormed out of the house and missed my bus to school. I knew that catching the next bus meant I would be late to my education class. That made me even more furious.

I fumed and sighed all the way to school. My mind raced with angry thoughts about my father. Like many adolescents, I was stuck in my egocentricity—certain that no one in the world had ever had such a terrible father or had to contend with such unfairness. After all, my father hadn't even finished high school, and here I was, a mighty college student! I felt so superior to him. How dare he interfere with my life and my plans?

As I ran across the sprawling campus toward the building where my class met, I suddenly realized that I didn't have the assignment that was due: a thought card.

This class was taught by Dr. Sidney B. Simon, one of the most unusual teachers at the school. His policies and procedures were unique, his grading policy revolutionary, his teaching methods unsettling. People talked about Dr. Simon.

During our first class, Professor Simon had explained, "Every Tuesday, you must bring in a four-by-six index card with your name and the date on the top line. As for what's on the rest of the card, that's up to you. You can write a thought, a concern, a feeling, a question or just plain anything that's on your mind. It's your way of communicating with me directly. These cards will be completely confidential. I will return them to you every Wednesday. You'll find that I will write comments on your cards. If you ask a question, I'll do my level best to answer it. If you have a concern, I will respond to that as best I can. But remember, this card is your admission ticket to class on Tuesdays."

On the first Tuesday of the class, I dutifully brought in my index card with my name and the date written carefully on the top line. I then added, "All that glitters is not gold." The following day, Dr. Simon returned the cards to the class. Mine had a penciled note: "What does this quote mean to you? Is it significant?" This comment made me uneasy. Apparently, he was taking these cards seriously. I surely didn't want to reveal myself to him.

The week progressed. The course met every day for one hour. Dr. Simon was quite brilliant. He taught by asking questions, raising issues that none of my teachers had ever raised before. He challenged us to think, and to think deeply. Social issues, political issues, personal issues all were grist for the mill in this class. It was a class in methods of teaching social studies, and it was far ranging. The teachers I had in high school taught social studies, history, geography, economics and so on, as rote subjects, lists of facts and names and dates to be memorized and returned to paper on exams. Rarely had anyone asked us to think.

At first, I thought he was going to propagandize us for or against something, but not Professor Simon. Instead, he simply asked us to think, explore, research, question and then come up with our own responses. Frankly, I became even more uncomfortable. There was something delightful, refreshing and inviting about his teaching, but since I had rarely experienced this style, I had no "coping strategies" to help me deal with him. I knew how to do well in a class: sit up front; tell the teacher how much you "enjoyed" the lecture; turn in neat, typed papers written according to a formula; and memorize, memorize, memorize! This class was clearly something different. I couldn't use these time-worn, time-tested methods to pass.

The second Tuesday came. I wrote on my card, "A stitch in time gathers no moss." Again, not trusting him, I covered myself with humor, which had always been my best defense against unwanted closeness. The next day the card came back with this note: "You seem to have a sense of humor. Is this an important part of your life?"

What did he want? What was going on here? I couldn't remember a teacher caring personally about me since elementary school. What did this man want?

Now, I raced down the hallway, ten minutes late to class. Just outside the door, I took an index card from my notebook and wrote my name and the date on it. Desperate for something to write on it, I could only think about the fight I'd just had with my dad. "I am the son of an idiot!" I wrote and then dashed into the room. He stood, conducting a discussion, near the door. Looking up at me, he reached out for the card, and I handed it to him and took my seat.

The moment I reached my seat, I felt overwhelmed with dread.

What had I done? I gave him that card! Oh, no! I didn't mean to let that out. Now he'll know about my anger, about my dad, about my life! I don't remember anything about the rest of that class session. All I could think about was the card.

I had difficulty sleeping that night, filled with a nameless dread. What could these cards be all about? Why did I tell him that about my dad? Suppose he contacts my dad? What business is it of his anyway?

Wednesday morning arrived, and I reluctantly got ready for school. When I got to the class, I was early. I wanted to sit in back and hide as best I could. The class began, and Dr. Simon began giving back the thought cards. He put mine on the desk facedown as was his usual practice. I picked it up, almost unable to turn it over.

When I looked at the face of the card, I discovered he had written, "What does the 'son of an idiot' do with the rest of his life?" It felt like someone had punched me in the stomach. I had spent a lot of time hanging out in the student union cafeteria talking with other young men about the problems I had "because of my parents." And they, too, shared the same sort of material with me. No one challenged anyone to take responsibility for themselves. No, we each accepted the others' blame-the-parents game with relief. It was all our parents' fault. If we did poorly on tests, blame Mom. If we just missed getting a student-aide job, blame Dad. I constantly complained about my folks, and all the guys nodded sagely. These folks who were paying the tuition were certainly an interfering bunch of fools, weren't they?

Sidney Simon's innocent-seeming question punctured that balloon. It got right to the heart of the issue: Whose problem is it? Whose responsibility are you?

I skipped going to the student union that day and went straight home, strangely depressed, chastened. All evening I thought about it and about something my mother had said: "The millionaire calls himself a 'self-made man,' but if he gets arrested, he blames his abusive parents."

I wish I could say that I experienced a magic transformation, but I didn't. However, Dr. Simon's comment was insidious. It kept coming up in my mind over the next few weeks. Again and again, as I heard myself blaming my father for this or that, a little internal voice said, "Okay, suppose your father is all those bad things you said. How long do you think you can get away with blaming him for your life?"

Slowly, inexorably, my thinking began to shift. I heard myself blaming a lot. After a while, I realized that I had created a life in which I was not a central figure! I was the object of the action, not the subject. That felt even more uncomfortable than any feeling I had in Dr. Simon's class. I didn't want to be a puppet. I wanted to be an actor, not a re-actor.

The process of growth wasn't easy or fast. It took over a year before people began to notice that I was taking responsibility for my own actions, my own choices, my own feelings. I was surprised at how my grades improved in all my subjects. I was astounded at the increase in the number—and quality—of my friends. It was equally astonishing how much smarter my father seemed.

All through this process, I kept sending in my thought cards. Later, I took another course with this unique professor. I worked harder for him than I had in any other class I had ever taken. With each thought card came more unsettling questions for thought.

Several years later, I was surprised at my own progress. From a struggling, marginal student, I had become a successful student and then a successful high school teacher. I went from constant anger and constant avoidance of the necessary work in my life to become someone who was energized, excited, purposeful and even joyful.

My relationship with my father also improved dramatically. Instead of controlling, now I saw him as concerned and caring. I recognized that he didn't have "smooth" ways of parenting me but that his intentions were very loving. The fights diminished and finally disappeared. I had learned to see my father as a smart, wise and loving man. And it all started with a question, an innocent-seeming question.

Hanoch McCarty

I Passed the Test

I was just eighteen years old when I entered nursing school, easily the youngest member of my class. Consequently, I was the subject of a great deal of teasing and good-natured ribbing from my classmates, many of whom were single mothers and older women returning to school for a second career.

Unfortunately, I became ill one week and missed a crucial test on the subject of mental health. This was particularly important to me since I planned to enter the mental-health field once I became a full-fledged nurse. Being a serious student, I immediately scheduled a time to re-test and began cramming for this exam. My fellow classmates knew how important this exam was to me and encouraged me as much as possible.

On the day of my test, as scheduled, I came to the classroom an hour early where one of my instructors administered the test. It was indeed a difficult exam, with more than one hundred questions pertaining to brain development and the latest trends in mental health. My intense study sessions served me well and, in less than forty minutes, I passed the test with flying colors.

Anxious to share my test results with my fellow students,

I ran to the hospital coffee shop where we students spent our free time with members of the hospital support staff. As soon as I entered the coffee shop, I cried out in a loud voice, "I passed my mental retardation test!"

As I looked around the busy coffee shop, I could not find any of my classmates. Instead, a group of maintenance men, with confused looks on their faces, rose to give me a standing ovation.

Paula Lopez-Crespin

Yes, Dad, I've passed English lit, and I'm now passing chemistry and physics.

The Wicker Chair

During my senior year in college, I took a marketing class taught by a cantankerous old man. On the first day of class, he made some predictions. First, he said we would always remember his name. Visualize a jack-o'-lantern in the seat of a wicker chair—and you will always remember Jack Wickert. Second, he said most people would fare very badly in this class because he had no patience with students who don't do the assignments and follow instructions. Last, there would be no more than three As out of the forty students in the class.

He made us sweat all semester. No doubt, we learned something about creative avenues for marketing products. He taunted and jeered at us and called us airheads. This was a night class. Everyone worked full-time. By 7:00 P.M., we were tired—imagine how we felt at 10:00 P.M. after being beaten up for three hours!

Mr. Wickert scheduled the final exam for the second-to-last week of the semester. We would review the results on the last night of class. On the night of the final exam, Jack Wickert told the class there was only one question. Then he stunned us all by announcing, "This is an open exam. You may look through your books, your notes or anything that will help. In fact, as far as I'm concerned, you may leave the room, go to the library, telephone your friends. You may do any research you like. There are a few things you may not do. You may not talk to or disturb anyone else in the class. You may not share your findings. And finally, don't bother me. When you finish, put your results on my desk and leave."

Then, Wickert proceeded to write the problem on the board: Develop a marketing plan for an electronic rattrap costing $150. (In 1977 dollars, that was the equivalent of one month's rent.)

About half the class immediately got up and left. I looked over at one of my friends. He arched his eyebrow, shrugged and shook his head. What a horrible thing to have to market. Who's going to spend a whole week's salary on one rattrap? If you really had rats, you were likely to be living in a slum and certainly couldn't afford this princely cost. If you could afford it, you lived where there were no infestations. And our grade depended on solving this problem.

I just sat there, staring at the blackboard. I knew there was a catch. What was the gimmick? Knowing Wickert, there was a trick to this. And the answer was easy. He just knew we'd be too dense to catch it. So, I sat there staring and thinking. Finally, I got it! The answer was clear. You couldn't sell it. Write the report, briefly explaining that this was not marketable, cut your losses, move on to something practical. So, I wrote it out on one page. I started packing up my things and looked up to catch Mr. Wickert looking at me with a smug, evil leer.

I stopped. I sat back down. If I handed it to him, it would be irrevocable. And his look told me that he thought he had won. He had outsmarted me. I sat there looking at him. He wouldn't look at me again. Now, he was just sitting there smiling broadly, pretending to read.

So, I was forced to reflect on the rats. The trap was so expensive—and big (we had the dimensions). Where would you even put this thing if you could afford to buy one? I contemplated the problem some more. And more. And more.

Slowly, I started to think about large warehouses, factories . . . places you store things, like food, like perishables, like paper (picture rats gnawing), like boxes, grains . . . industrial facilities. Yes! Keep going. What else? Stores, supermarkets, restaurants. They could afford this. I was starting to get excited. Yes, they've got room to place this unwieldy device somewhere. Several places, in fact.

But it could cut into the revenues of exterminators. Yes! Exterminators, what a great market. They could buy them and sell them to their customers. Heck, they could rent them and collect huge profits. And off I went. That night, I developed a twenty-page marketing plan. It was logical, reasonable and feasible.

I was quite satisfied with my marketing plan. Just before 10:00 P.M., I dropped it on his desk. He was still looking smug, but what the heck. I had tried.

Next Wednesday, he showed up in class with the results. He announced, "You met my lowest expectations. Most of you missed the whole point, and your grades reflect it. However, I am annoyed. I was forced to grant one more A than I had predicted." And he glared pointedly at me. "There were four this semester."

He handed out the graded finals. The groans and grumbling were audible. However, I had gotten an A. Why did I sense he wasn't going to let me enjoy it?

Wickert interrupted all the complaints. "I warned you at the beginning of class that you would not do the assignments or read the book. You took the lazy way out—and it cost you. If you had followed my instructions, this final would have been a slam dunk. Now that it's over, I can tell you. I took the case straight out of the textbook. Verbatim. I did not even bother to change the name on the case. I knew you wouldn't notice."

You could hear the sound of pages rustling as we frantically searched the textbook and the index, looking for the case. Then, there was dead silence as we read it. Oddly enough, the case's marketing plan turned out to be very similar to my own. They thought up a few things that I hadn't and vice versa.

"I was confident in you dunderheads. Only three people figured out what I had done during the final and took the information out of the book." (He had been watching us and knew who'd used the book. I hadn't even cracked mine. He was right.) "But one person did it the hard way and actually reasoned it out on her own. It would have saved her a lot of time if she had just done what I had asked."

Yes, it would have saved me time—and embarrassment. But, I did figure it out myself, although I hadn't followed his directions. I had thought it through and come up with the correct answer. Could Wickert have been trying to goad us young students into thinking?

Even to this day I wonder if Wickert was secretly proud of me, as well.

Eva Rosenberg

Dissed

Chad was intimidated by the burly professor yelling into his face, "Your work is sloppy! Your study habits are horrible! Your grades are slipping! I hate sloppy work! I hate poor study habits! And I hate that shirt you are wearing!"

The class was dead silent as the professor chastised Chad for several minutes. Then a collective gasp filled the room when the professor turned and began to yell at the entire class.

"You guys have made it through high school because your mommies babied you. Now you have to grow up! Your mommies are not *here!*"

Chad spoke in a quivering voice. "You'd better be glad my mom's not here. *She* bought me this shirt!"

Mary J. Davis

How to Get an A on Your Final Exam

During my senior year in college, I served as a teacher's assistant. One of my roles was to administer and proctor the exams. The class was a freshman introductory course, which had well over five hundred students.

The students were given four exams during the semester and one cumulative final exam at the semester's end. In order to manage these five hundred college freshmen, I had to establish rules. The rules were as follows. The exams began at exactly 9:00 A.M. The students would pick up their test booklets and blue books and proceed to a seat of their choosing. They would have exactly fifty minutes to complete the examination. At exactly 9:50 A.M., I would call out, "Pencils down!" Everyone had to stop writing immediately, put their pencils down, proceed to the front of the room and turn in their blue books. Those who did not put their pencils down at exactly 9:50 A.M. and turn in their blue books would receive an automatic F, no exceptions!

When final exam time came, the students were so indoctrinated into the system that I only needed to announce one warning at 9:40 A.M. So as the final minutes ticked away, I announced, "It is 9:40. You have ten minutes until pencils down." Then at 9:50 A.M., I barked my last command for that semester: "It's 9:50, pencils down. You know the rules!" And boom, all pencils went down, just like always. All 500 students stood—or was it only 499? Yes it was. Everyone filled the aisle except for one sneaky guy—a guy way up in the nosebleed section.

He was just writing and writing away. I saw him up there, but he didn't think I could. Once again, I barked, "Pencils down everyone!" But he kept writing and writing, trying to beat my system. How dare he! Boy, would I get him! At 9:58 A.M., as I began to organize the stacks of examination packets, I saw this young man running down the aisle to surrender his exam to the table.

"Here, Mr. D'Angelo, take my blue book!" he huffed and puffed.

"I cannot accept this. You know the rules. Pencils down at 9:50 A.M., or you get an automatic F."

"Please, Mr. D'Angelo, take my blue book!"

"*No!* You know I can't do that. It's against the rules."

"Please, please, take my blue book. I'm barely passing this class. My mom and dad will kill me if I have to repeat this class. Just take it, and no one will ever know." A tear began to stream down his cheek.

"I'm sorry. I just can't." I went back to the stacks, organizing them one by one. The young man just turned and walked away with his shoulders slumped.

Now with a stack of five hundred or so blue books in my arms, I watched the freshman walk up the stairs toward the exit. Just about at the halfway point, I saw him boldly turn around, with great confidence, you might say with a hint of arrogance. He swiftly jogged down to me.

He questioned softly, "Mr. D'Angelo, do you know who I am?"

"Why no, and frankly I couldn't care less."

"Are you sure you don't know who I am?" he inquired with even greater confidence. I started to get a little concerned. Was this the dean's son? What had I gotten myself into?

"No, I'm sorry. I don't," I said with a little hesitation in my voice.

"Are you absolutely, 100 percent sure that you don't know who I am?"

"For the last time, no, I don't know who you are!"

"Well then, good!" and he shoved his blue book into the middle of the stack and ran out the door.

Tony D'Angelo

Is it too late to drop the course?

Reprinted by permission of Harley Schwadron.

A Compassionate Philosophy

A half hour before test time, I was afraid to look in the mirror. But I had to assess the damages. After all, there were cute guys in this class. Granted, they would be worrying more about the final than what I looked like, and that was my hope at this point.

The first things I saw were my own bloodshot eyes. Where was that Visine? My hair looked like Attila the Hun had spent the night camping in it. Well, I'd pull it back into a ponytail and take the tangles out later.

And then I saw it. It was a huge swelling on the front of my chin that had to be the size of a small golf ball. Surely I was hallucinating from lack of sleep. I had never seen anything like that before. I'd heard of people getting hives from nerves. But a single hive, on the front of my face? I gingerly touched it. A hard swelling met my curious fingertips. What had caused this? The pizza I'd consumed at midnight or the Mountain Dew I'd consumed at two and four and six in the morning? Perhaps it was the Cap'n Crunch at three or the candy bar at five. My stomach had a strict policy. If I was going to keep it up all night, it insisted on being fed.

How was I going to cover this up? I rummaged through all of my toiletries until I found my lone bandage, put there for emergencies. Well, this qualified as one. Oh no, that looked really stupid. How embarrassing. Oh well, no time to do anything else about it now. My philosophy final was waiting for me. My beleaguered brain had tried all night to grasp the arguments of different philosophies so that I could write them down on the essay test this morning.

I loved to hear our philosophy professor in class. I could follow the arguments when he discussed them, but trying to formulate them on my own just wasn't happening. Perhaps the bump was the result of stress. I had to pass this final, or I would fail the class. And I couldn't fail the class, or I would have to take the college's summer school sessions. And I couldn't go to summer school because I needed to work to help pay for next fall's tuition.

Swallowing the last gulp of flat Mountain Dew, I headed for class. I picked a seat that didn't directly face the clock. That would only make me more nervous, and God knew I had already used up my adrenaline supply. Dr. Wennberg passed out the essay books while explaining the rules. We would have exactly one hour. My two pencils in hand, I waited for the signal.

"Begin."

I closed my eyes, took a deep breath and said a prayer: "Please, God, help me remember all that I've studied for this test."

I looked over the questions. I could do this. I had to do this. I began writing.

Twenty minutes had gone by. I had been writing as fast as I could before I forgot the information. So far so good. But my eyes were so tired. They hurt so badly. They felt so heavy. I'd just rest them for a minute. I leaned my puffy chin on my hand.

Someone sneezed. I came to with a start. What?! I'd fallen asleep? I'd never done that before in a final! Oh no!

Fearfully, I looked at the clock. Only ten minutes left?! I'd slept a half hour? Oh *no!*

I thought I'd used up all my adrenaline, but I was wrong. I broke out in a cold sweat. What could I do in ten minutes? Think, I must think. I need a plan. I'm doomed. No, think. I began writing as fast as I could to finish answering the questions.

I stared at the last blank page of the essay test booklet with its neatly ruled lines. Dare I? I had nothing to lose. I still had two minutes. I wrote Dr. Wennberg. I told him how sorry I was. How I'd stayed awake all night to study because this was important to me, only to fall asleep during the exam. How I'd really wanted to do better. I asked for mercy.

One week later, I stood in front of the test board where the results would be posted. The mysterious swelling on my chin had gone away with sleep, but I touched my fingers to my chin nervously. It wasn't coming back, was it?

I stood awaiting my fate. The secretary came out and pinned a paper to the board. I scanned down the list of names, looking for my final class grade. There it was: a C-minus. Tears filled my eyes. I looked again. I had passed! I was sure I hadn't deserved that. But I wasn't about to argue! Dr. Wennberg had shown mercy. It was one philosophy lesson I've never forgotten.

Kristi Nay

You know, I just might pass that chemistry
test after all. . . .

Reprinted by permission of Dave Carpenter.

Library Science

It was only the third week of our domestic union, and already I had major doubts about my new roommate. And not just because of the psychedelic unicorn triptych tacked over her bed or the Garfield phone staring at me from her trunk. She was hiding something, I could tell.

I knew for a fact that her first class wasn't until 11:00 A.M., but she was out the door by nine every morning. With her books. She'd stay out all day, not even showing up for *Days of Our Lives*, unlike the rest of us who had deliberately designed our schedules around this sacred hour.

I began to speculate about how and where she was spending her time. I knew that she had taken out loans to pay for tuition; maybe she was hanging out at the plasma center—rumor had it they paid you a hundred bucks to donate blood. Maybe she was having an affair with one of her professors. Maybe she'd never signed up for classes and was going to the movies all day. Finally, I couldn't stand it any longer. I had to know what was up.

"Lori, I was just wondering . . . where exactly do you go all day?"

She didn't even flinch. "The library."

The what? What could she possibly be doing in the library all day? We were only freshmen. It's not like she was writing a thesis or anything. I wasn't so sure I believed her.

"Can I go with you tomorrow?" I asked, waiting for her to squirm as she was forced to blow her cover.

"Sure," she said easily.

So that's where we went. At first glance, it looked exactly like what I'd expected: a bunch of people sitting around reading and being systematically shushed. But upon closer inspection, I realized the library is a lot like one of those "Magic Eye" pictures that hypnotize mallgoers everywhere—if you look hard enough, you discover there's a lot more to it. For one thing, it's an excellent hiding spot.

Imagine this scenario: Last night it seemed like a good idea to use your suitemate's cherished (but handy) Green Day T-shirt to plug the leak in the toilet tank. Today, you're slightly less sure. Well, good thing for you the library is always open late. Just drape the tee over your chair, kick back and hit the books. Later, when you sneak the no-longer-incriminating evidence back into your undersized cell, you'll be home free.

And speaking of free, this is one of the few campus hot spots with no cover charge and no minimum. You can read as much as you want! Study all day! All for the incredibly low price that is music to any college student's ears: notta (as in notta penny—unless you permanently misplace *Moby Dick* and have to dig into your precious laundry fund to replace it).

Dreading the weekly bad-news report from Mom? Even if she knows where you are, chances are she won't page you in the library. Having a hard time losing the geek from your dorm who won't stop calling since you accidentally made eye contact? You're as good as lost.

The word "dorm" is definitely not short for "dormant." That place makes a mosh pit look tame! Phones ringing,

stereos blasting, computers humming, video games bleep-
ing, TVs blaring—it'd be easier to think in an arcade. What
you wouldn't give for three minutes of peace and quiet.

Voilà! You've come to the right place. Write a letter.
Read the newspaper. Skim a few chapters. Or just sit and
make like a vegetable. Who cares? Your only purpose is to
suck up the divine silence.

It sounds good: "Going to the library."

Your parents will be impressed. Your professors will be
impressed. Your friends will be, well, already there. Of
course, the former groups will assume you're there studying, which you may or may not be doing. It doesn't really
matter, though, since they won't ever think to ask.

Therefore, the library can become your sanctuary, the
place to do whatever it is you feel like doing (excluding, of
course, your full-volume Stimpy impression and the
Native American war dance you just learned about in history) under the guise of higher education.

Bonus incentive: When you get back to your dorm,
your answering machine and e-mail box will both be
jammed with messages because everyone knows that
people only try to contact you when you're out.

Not to mention the boy-watching. Granted, there aren't
many on-campus places that aren't conducive to a
rewarding game of I Spy, but the library may be one of the
best. Why? Because the guys, like the books, are often cate-
gorized by type. Before long, with one quick scan of the
room, you'll be able to determine who's there to scam, to
cram or to find out when and where the next big party is.

If you're serious about acing your organic-chem
final—but aren't willing to deprive yourself of visual
pleasure—plunk your stuff down in the carrel ("library-
speak" for private study table) with a clear view of that
industrious premed student you've noticed lurking
around the science building. You'll get to sneak a few

well-deserved peeks, and he'll be too wrapped up in mammalian fetal anatomy to notice.

On the other hand, if you'd rather tap into the social scene than analyze the complete works of Ezra Pound, avoid the floors crammed with carrels and go straight to the group-study tables. Not only are you guaranteed not to get a moment's work done there, you might even wind up with a date.

You can study there, too. Sort of obvious, but some people have mental blocks when it comes to intended use. The library, you see, has a few distinct advantages over some other potential study spots, like, say, your couch or the campus pool. First of all, the required posture in this place is upright. In other words, no "I'll just stretch out on this extra-quilted mattress and read a few chapters." Trust me, there's little risk of drifting off—no matter how boring your English assignment—when you're propped up in a standard-issue posture-friendly chair. It's practically proven: Your grades will improve dramatically if you're awake during the bulk of your study time.

Second, the library has stuff. I mean, sure, it has books. Millions of them, in fact. But in addition to racks of hardbacks, libraries are also jammed with these amazing things called resources, like copy machines, computers, desks, magazines, microfilm and kind, helpful people known as reference librarians (otherwise known as The Ones Who Actually Have Answers).

Yeah, yeah, life is short, and college is shorter. Who wants to spend all that time kissing up to a librarian? I can personally promise you this will not be a waste of your wonder years. Even after your final exam, you'll probably still hit the library from time to time. You might be looking for a job, filing your taxes or just trying to hunt down a good read. Or maybe you heard Prenatal Pig Guy is studying for his boards or researching which hospitals are looking for brilliant residents with chiseled features. Whatever the case, you can bet you'll be back inside a library one day soon. Might as well know your way around.

Jenna McCarthy

Your Legacy

I had a philosophy professor who was the quintessential eccentric philosopher. His disheveled appearance was highlighted by a well-worn tweed sport coat and poor-fitting thick glasses, which often rested on the tip of his nose. Every now and then, as most philosophy professors do, he would go off on one of those esoteric and existential "what's the meaning of life" discussions. Many of those discussions went nowhere, but there were a few that really hit home. This was one of them:

"Respond to the following questions by a show of hands," my professor instructed.

"How many of you can tell me something about your parents?" Everyone's hand went up.

"How many of you can tell me something about your grandparents?" About three-fourths of the class raised their hands.

"How many of you can tell me something about your great-grandparents?" Two out of sixty students raised their hands.

"Look around the room," he said. "In just two short generations hardly any of us even know who our own great-grandparents were. Oh sure, maybe we have an old, tattered photograph tucked away in a musty cigar box or know the classic family story about how one of them walked five miles to school barefoot. But how many of us really know who they were, what they thought, what they were proud of, what they were afraid of, or what they dreamed about? Think about that. Within three generations our ancestors are all but forgotten. Will this happen to you?

"Here's a better question. Look ahead three generations. You are long gone. Instead of you sitting in this room, now it's your great-grandchildren. What will they have to say about you? Will they know about you? Or will you be forgotten, too?

"Is your life going to be a warning or an example? What legacy will you leave? The choice is yours. Class dismissed."

Nobody rose from their seat for a good five minutes.

Tony D'Angelo

Angels on a Pin
(101 Ways to Use a Barometer)

Some time ago I received a call from a colleague, who asked if I would be the referee on the grading of an examination question. He was about to give a student a zero for his answer to a physics question, while the student claimed he should receive a perfect score and would if the system were not set up against the student. The instructor and the student agreed to an impartial arbiter, and I was selected.

I went to my colleague's office and read the examination question: "Show how it is possible to determine the height of a tall building with the aid of a barometer."

The student had answered: "Take the barometer to the top of the building, attach a long rope to it, lower it to the street, and then bring it up, measuring the length of the rope. The length of the rope is the height of the building."

I pointed out that the student really had a strong case for full credit since he had really answered the question completely and correctly. On the other hand, if full credit were given, it could well contribute to a high grade in his physics course. A high grade is supposed to certify competence in physics, but the answer did not confirm this. I suggested that the student have another try at answering the question. I was not surprised that my colleague agreed, but I was surprised when the student did.

I gave the student six minutes to answer the question with the warning that the answer should show some knowledge of physics. At the end of five minutes, he had not written anything. I asked if he wished to give up, but he said no. He had many answers to this problem; he was just thinking of the best one. I excused myself for interrupting him and asked him to please go on. In the next minute he dashed off his answer which read: "Take the barometer to the top of the building and lean over the edge. Drop the barometer, timing its fall with a stopwatch. Then, using the formula $S = \frac{1}{2}AT^2$, calculate the height of the building."

At this point, I asked my colleague if he would give up. He conceded, and gave the student almost full credit.

In leaving my colleague's office, I recalled the student had said that he had other answers to the problem, so I asked him what they were.

"Well," said the student, "there are many ways of getting the height of a tall building with the aid of a barometer. For example, you could take the barometer out on a sunny day and measure the height of the barometer, the length of its shadow, and the length of the shadow of the building, and, by the use of simple proportion, determine the height of the building."

"Fine," I said, "any others?"

"Yes," said the student. "There is a very basic measurement method you will like. In this method, you take the barometer and begin to walk up the stairs. As you climb the stairs, you mark off the length of the barometer along the wall. You then count the number of marks, and this will give you the height of the building in barometer units. A very direct method.

"Of course, if you want a more sophisticated method, you can tie the barometer to the end of a string, swing it as a pendulum and determine the value of g at the street level and at the top of the building. From the difference between the two values of g, the height of the building, in principle, can be calculated.

"On this same tack, you could take the barometer to the top of the building, attach a long rope to it, lower it to just above the street and then swing it as a pendulum. You could then calculate the height of the building by the period of the precession.

"Finally, there are many other ways of solving the problem," he concluded. "Probably the best is to take the barometer to the basement and knock on the superintendent's door. When the superintendent answers, you speak to him as follows: 'Mr. Superintendent, here is a fine barometer. If you will tell me the height of the building, I will give you this barometer.'"

At this point, I asked the student if he really did not know the conventional answer to this question. He admitted that he did, but said that he was fed up with college instructors trying to teach him how to think.

Alexander Calandra
Submitted by Kelly Steinhaus

Topsy-Turvy World

I have often wondered why we are asked to focus so much on what is wrong and so little on what is right. I think that if we changed our focus and concentrated on what is right we would have a much better outcome.

Imagine your teacher hands back your test and he or she says, "Let's go over the questions you answered correctly." They might say, for instance, "Kim, that was a brilliant answer you gave to question number three" or "Brian, number six was some of your finest work ever." I can't help but think I would leave that class with a little spring in my step.

I love this conversation between Alice and the Mad Hatter, excerpted from Lewis Carroll's *Alice in Wonderland*:

> Alice: *Where I come from, people study what they are not good at in order to be able to do what they are good at.*
>
> Mad Hatter: *We only go around in circles in Wonderland, but we always end up where we started. Would you mind explaining yourself?*

Alice: *Well, grown-ups tell us to find out what we did wrong, and never do it again.*

Mad Hatter: *That's odd! It seems to me that in order to find out about something, you have to study it. And when you study it, you should become better at it. Why should you want to become better at something and then never do it again? But please continue.*

Alice: *Nobody ever tells us to study the right things we do. We're only supposed to learn from the wrong things. But we are permitted to study the right things other people do. And sometimes we're even told to copy them.*

Mad Hatter: *That's cheating!*

Alice: *You're quite right, Mr. Hatter. I do live in a topsy-turvy world. It seems like I have to do something wrong first, in order to learn from what not to do. And then, by not doing what I'm not supposed to do, perhaps I'll be right. But I'd rather be right the first time, wouldn't you?*

Kimberly Kirberger

4

LESSONS FROM OUTSIDE THE CLASSROOM

If A *is success in life, then* A *equals* X *plus* Y *plus* Z. *Work is* X, Y *is play and* Z *is keeping your mouth shut.*

Albert Einstein

College Wisdom Seldom Exercised in the Summer

It's time once again for college students to be reminded of the Law of Diminishing Tuition Fruition.

This is the law that says: "The twenty thousand dollars you spent on your education this past year renders you *worthless in the real world* this summer."

Mother Nature reminds college students of this law each May through a phenomenon called "the summer job."

The summer job has two purposes. It allows the college student to earn one-millionth of the money he'll be needing to get through the next school year. And it reminds him that he's got absolutely nothing on the ball as far as Summer Job Bosses are concerned.

I had more summer jobs than I care to remember. I was a maid, a waitress, a telephone operator, a waitress, a salesperson, a waitress, a clerk, a waitress and a waitress another six or so times.

The odd thing was, it didn't matter what the job was because I always did the same thing: *I always did whatever no one else wanted to do!*

As a resort waitress one summer, it was my job to make

the orange juice in the morning. This wasn't just ordinary orange juice. It came in cans the size of driveway-sealer containers that I believe were stored on Pluto to make sure the juice was definitely and thoroughly frozen.

My work involved making orange juice with a sledge hammer. After two weeks, when I began looking like Hulk Hogan, I decided to *make a suggestion.* This made me nervous, but I took the chance, as I was so big and strong by then.

"Wouldn't it be easier to defrost this stuff the night before?" I said.

"What are you, a college wise guy?" sneered the boss. "We serve *fresh* frozen orange juice here, not *defrosted* frozen orange juice. Now bang on it."

Probably the worst summer job I ever had was the year I was the Wink Girl.

Wink was a soft drink during the 1960s that never made it. My job was to dress up in an outfit that looked like a Wink can—a lime green skirt and yellow polyester top—and promote the product by driving around with the Wink Man in the Wink Truck.

I never knew where the Wink Man came from. He looked like the type of gentleman who knew where a lot of bodies were buried in landfills. I always suspected he was given the identity of Wink Man under the Federal Witness Protection Program after he squealed on "the boss." Anyway, he just drifted into the local employment office one day looking for a Wink Girl.

Our job was to stop the Wink Truck wherever there might be thirsty people so that the Wink Girl—me—could give out free samples of Wink while the Wink Man—him—studied his racing form in the truck.

On my first day, the Wink Man had a problem with my performance. We were parked in front of a high school as summer school let out, and I was pouring little samples as fast as my spigot could handle.

The Wink Man called me around the front of the truck.

"Wink," he said.

"What?" I said.

"You have to wink when you give out the soda," he said. "It's part of the job."

"But young boys consider winking an invitation of sorts," I said.

"What are you, a college wise guy?" he sneered. "You're the Wink Girl. You wink."

So I went back and began winking at high school boys. All that summer I winked at teenagers, old ladies, construction workers and small children. My left eye was exhausted by the end of each day, but I had a lot of dates.

My own boy is going through this summer-job ordeal right now. Last summer, his job was "mudbuster."

"That's my title," he told me when he got the job. "Mudbuster."

At work, he asked for an explanation of his duties.

"What's the job description?" he asked. "I mean, what does a mudbuster do?"

"Go over there and bust up that mud, boy," the boss told him.

"Why?" asked my boy.

"What are you, a college wise guy?" he sneered. "You think you're too good for busting mud?"

"No, sir," said my boy, who was taught to be respectful of all life forms. "It's just that a worker is generally more productive when he understands the purpose of his task."

"Bust the mud," said his boss. My boy busted a mountain of mud that summer, and he never did learn what the boss wanted it for.

I don't know what he'll be doing this summer, but I figure he's qualified to be a waiter—as long as his duties are limited to busting orange juice.

Beth Mullally

Learning How to Be Roommates

I was never very neat. Later in life I learned to attribute this flaw to my creative genius, saying that my bouts of disorganization were simply the flip side of my unique gifts and talents. Yet, when I arrived at college, I hadn't come up with any impressive reasons for my big messes. They just *were*—and my roommate didn't seem to appreciate their contribution to my bright future.

I'm not sure why they stuck us together. I don't think they could have possibly picked two more different people to room together. Kim was extremely organized. She labeled everything and each item she owned had its place. She even had one of those cute little pencil holders— and used it! Mine had become a collection spot for bits and pieces of paper, odds and ends. I think one pen may have found its way into the pencil holder but I certainly didn't put it there.

Kim and I fed off each other. She got neater and I got messier. She would complain about my dirty clothes, I would complain about Lysol headaches. She would nudge my clothing over to one side and I would lay one of my books on her uncluttered desk.

It came to a head one fateful October evening. Kim

came into the room and had some kind of fit because one of my shoes had found its way (inexplicably) beneath her bed. I don't know what was so significant about that shoe but it infuriated her! She picked it up, tossed it toward my side of the room and managed to knock my lamp onto the floor. The lightbulb shattered, covering the layer of clothes I had been planning to fold that very night. I leapt off the bed in horror and immediately started yelling about her insensitivity and rudeness. She yelled back similar frustrations and we each ended up pushing toward the door to be the first to slam our way out of the room.

I'm sure we wouldn't have lasted a day or two longer in that room. Probably not even a night, if it hadn't been for the phone call she received. I was sitting on my bed, fuming. She was sitting on hers, fuming. It was later in the evening and the room was so thick with unspoken expletives that I don't even know why we had both returned to each other's company.

When the phone rang she picked it up and I could tell right away it wasn't good news. I knew Kim had a boyfriend back home and I could tell from her end of the conversation that he was breaking up with her. Though I didn't mean for it to happen, I could feel the warm feelings of empathy rising up in my heart. Losing a boyfriend was something no girl should go through alone.

I sat up in my bed. Kim wouldn't look at me and when she hung up the phone she quickly crawled under her covers and I could hear her quiet sobbing. What to do? I didn't want to just walk over (I was still a little miffed) but I didn't want to leave her either. I smiled as I got the idea.

Slowly, I began to clear up my side of the room. I took back the book I had set on her desk and I cleaned up the socks and the shirts. I put some pencils in my pencil holder and made my bed. I straightened the dresser top (but not the drawers—I had my limits!) and swept the floor, even on her side. I got so into my work that I didn't even notice that Kim had come out from under the covers. She was watching my every move, her tears dried and her expression one of disbelief. When I was finally done I went and sat at the end of her bed. Not really saying anything but just sitting. I guess I didn't know what to say. Her hand was warm. I thought it would be cold, probably because I always thought the organized were pretty heartless. But no. Her hand was warm as it reached over to grasp mine. I looked up into Kim's eyes and she smiled at me. "Thanks."

Kim and I stayed roommates for the rest of that year. We didn't always see eye to eye, but we learned the key to living together. Giving in, cleaning up and holding on.

Elsa Lynch

Well, Mom, I met my new roommate today.
He has at least 3,827 bad habits . . . but after
five minutes I stopped counting.

The Plaster Shell

Intense feelings of embarrassment and absurdity filled my entire body. These feelings were not helped by the fact that I was slathered in baby oil, clad in a T-shirt and lying in my basement, in fifty pounds of plaster. I stared down at the warm plaster that embraced my midsection and slowly crept up toward my chest, and I tried to remember why I had chosen to make a plaster cast of my entire body. For a moment, I simply concluded that I was an utter fool, but I soon remembered my motives. And while the plaster dried, I certainly had the time to think about it.

The insecurities of my freshman year in college, combined with my poor body image, made me feel like an oaf. Here I was surrounded by all these lithe, long girls who wore the latest fashions really well. Was there some mold that churned out these girls? And where in the world did I come from?

That was the beginning of the question that led me to my plaster ensconcement. It all began 506 years ago, when my forebears were thrown out of Spain. They migrated to Eastern Europe and developed the stocky, bosomy shape consigned to overstuffed chairs. Though my tall, slender parents seemed to have defeated this pernicious (certainly in my eyes) shape, it continued lurking in the depths of the family gene pool and flung itself into existence again with the arrival of their firstborn child—me. It gifted me with wide hips, a nonexistent waistline, powerful shoulders and ample breasts. Very reminiscent of a long line of intimidating German matriarchs.

Built to survive harsh winters and to breed children, I certainly wasn't near anything I saw in fashion magazines —or like any of my new college peers. I loathed my shape and cursed my past. Though I was always an independent person who disregarded the edicts of popularity and fashion, I could not ignore our culture's concepts of beauty. The rancor I had for my body made my freshman year of college really hard. Clothing seemed made for those generic stick figures I sat next to in class. That was when Dorothy, my slightly eccentric art teacher and mentor, originated the idea of body casting.

Consequently, on a lovely May morning, I found myself sitting in a dark basement, encased in plaster. I lost all sensation in my legs at approximately the same time that the plaster hardened. After an additional uncomfortable twenty minutes, I slipped out of my plaster shell. At first, I was rather depressed by the sight of the powder-white and headless torso lying on an old towel. It looked more like a sea creature stranded by the tide than a human shape. My eyes squinted, trying not to take in the entire picture of my shape, which was even more exaggerated by the plaster. I thought about how I would never be graceful or delicate, how two-piece swimsuits were absolutely out of the question and how I would never be conventionally beautiful or fashionably thin.

As I stared at the empty outer shell of myself, a great realization hit me—I realized that I had been completely wrong about my body image. For the past nineteen years, I had believed that my linebacker-like shape would discourage others from noticing my additional attributes. How would they ever see my love of science and books, my creativity or my offbeat sense of humor?

All this time I had wanted to be fashionably svelte, but that would not make me a better person. I recognized that confidence was much more important to others than a dainty appearance and that if I had confidence, they would notice my talents. More important, I realized that I did not actually want to be thin and bikini-clad. I was quite content using my powerful build to lug around sixty-pound scenery pieces, and I liked my one-piece, practical bathing suits. My physical appearance had shaped my personality in a largely positive way. It contributed to my dislike of conformity. It gave me my somewhat self-deprecating sense of humor. And it gave me that strong will that I cherish so much. The misconception I was holding all these years, along with the exaggerated body cast that lay there on my basement floor, was suddenly so hilarious to me. I laughed for five minutes straight.

The body cast currently resides in Dorothy's attic, under a large blanket. I never actually used it in any art piece; I felt it had served its purpose. The process of body casting had been far more important than the product.

Since that day three years ago, I have not resented my ancestral build. I have also discovered that being comfortable in my body has given me increased confidence and assertiveness, something many girls, and women, lack. Perhaps they should all be given the opportunity to make their own body casts. When the shell of the body is separate from the person, it is obvious that it is severely lacking. Without the wisdom, sense of humor and heart, it really has no shape at all.

Miriam Goldstein

The Great Escape

I never felt like I could be myself in high school. I thought I had no choice: either I played cute, or boys wouldn't talk to me. So I hid my grades, kept my love for T. S. Eliot to myself and spoke in short sentences ("Good game," for example), biding my time until I could get to a place where everything would be different.

College, I knew, would be just that—the great escape to a place where everyone would talk fast, love books, stay up all night and not obsess about football. A chance to throw off the cheerleading uniform and let the real, witty, sophisticated me break free from my fake self. So I moved two thousand miles away from my tiny coal-mining town in western Colorado to attend Columbia University in New York City—the capital of fast-talking, book-reading weirdos.

But when I got to Columbia, the witty, sophisticated me, instead of bursting free, dove for cover. Everyone in New York seemed either insane or awesomely together. I couldn't imagine whom to hang out with or where I fit in. A girl in my hall raved about the rowing crew, so I declared that I would join. But when it came time to get up at 5:30 A.M. for a swimming test, I bailed. Then I went to a sorority rush event and realized that pledging meant wearing pearls—

so I split. Finally, I closed my eyes and jumped headlong into the hipster scene. I got a crew cut, bleached it blond, bought black clothes and dated an actor who claimed to have once stolen Ethan Hawke's girlfriend.

But somehow nothing quite worked. There's not a lot you can do with a crew cut, and black clothes get gloomy after six months straight. Plus, the actor continued to steal other people's girlfriends—while he was dating me. I tried to throw myself into my schoolwork, but my classes were so huge and formal that I was afraid to open my mouth. So there I was—still the same confused person in spite of my new surroundings.

But when I least expected it, things turned around. I started waitressing at a local café and met my soon-to-be best friend. We spent all our spare time there, studying and hanging out even when we weren't hawking fat-free cranberry muffins. Inside the café, I found a more casual atmosphere. A few of my professors came by regularly, and, perhaps because I was the one behind the espresso machine, we had the kind of relaxed, interesting conversations I'd imagined in high school. I found a close circle of friends. Another waitress and I started writing stories we called *The Adventures of Shark* and *Desperate Girl*, chronicling the paranoid behavior of two café regulars having a torrid, not-so-secret affair. I began to learn the fine art of flirting with the firemen who came in for java breaks and, finally, realized that I liked my life.

So college is the perfect place to find—or redo—yourself. Suddenly, without parents and high-school friends who remember when you tripped down the stairs at junior prom, it's a level playing field. The time is ripe to explore that long-concealed interest in pre-Cambrian fossils or to date a goateed poet type.

But once you have the chance to be anything you want, you face the really tough question: What do you want?

It's harder than it sounds. What you think you want when you're surrounded by familiar faces looks different in a new place. Things you thought were cool suddenly appear dorky, irrelevant or simply wrong. In high school, I was sure I'd fall in love with the first man who wanted to talk about Hemingway; but when I met that person, I hated his guts. I thought I'd find my voice in a college classroom; but in the end I was much happier scribbling down my thoughts and discussing them in the relaxed atmosphere of a coffee shop.

In other words, if you yearn to be someone quite unlike your high-school self, be fearless. Try whatever you can imagine until you find something that really fits. But in the meantime, go easy on yourself and others who are shopping for a new identity. I remember cattily criticizing a very straightlaced friend who had bought herself a motorcycle jacket. "How tacky," I told someone. "She's trying to look so tough, and she's so premed."

"You got a crew cut and dyed it blond," another friend pointed out.

Yeah, I thought, *I did. Maybe I should give her a break.*

After all, my friends and family gave me many breaks. They knew—even when I didn't—that somewhere amid all these shifting ambitions and new outfits, the same person still existed. And at graduation, as I was looking around the campus—my hair had almost grown out—it finally became clear to me why I'd come all these miles. It wasn't to become a completely different person. It was simply to figure out how to be comfortable with the person I was—not only at a huge university in an edgy city, but inside my own skin.

Wendy Marston

Hanging Out to Dry

The straight-laced theology student raced home and quickly parked in her garage. Her mission was to hang the wet wash to dry in the garage and make it back to class before her break ended.

She smiled as she hung up the last of the wash. *Made it,* she thought, proud of her ability to handle more than one thing at a time. She climbed in her car and headed back to class. As she waited at the red light, she thought about her final exams. But a feeling of being watched caused her to glance to her right. The young man in the vehicle parallel to hers gave her a devilish smile and winked at her repeatedly. Then he pointed to her car and winked three more times.

Her back stiffened and she stared ahead. The light turned green and the young man raced off. *Was he trying to pick me up?* she thought as she shook her head with disbelief.

After many strange looks in her direction, she pulled her car over and checked the tires. Then she spotted the problem. *Oh, my goodness,* she thought. *No wonder he had the wrong idea.* She then pulled her dangling wet bra from the antenna.

Paul Karrer

Wranglers and Stranglers

Years ago, a group of brilliant young men at the University of Wisconsin seemed to have amazing creative literary talent. They were would-be poets, novelists and essayists. They were extraordinary in their ability to put the English language to its best use. These promising young men met regularly to read and critique each other's work. And critique it they did!

These men were merciless with one another. They dissected the most minute literary expression into a hundred pieces. They were heartless, tough, even mean in their criticism. The sessions became such arenas of literary criticism that the members of this exclusive club called themselves the "Stranglers."

Not to be outdone, the women of literary talent in the university were determined to start a club of their own, one comparable to the Stranglers. They called themselves the "Wranglers." They, too, read their works to one another. But there was one great difference. The criticism was much softer, more positive, more encouraging. Sometimes, there was almost no criticism at all. Every effort, even the most feeble one, was encouraged.

Twenty years later, when an alumnus of the university

conducted an exhaustive study of his classmates' careers, he noticed a vast difference in the literary accomplishments of the Stranglers as opposed to the Wranglers. Of all the bright young men in the Stranglers, not one had made a significant literary accomplishment of any kind. From the Wranglers had come six or more successful writers, some of national renown, such as Marjorie Kinnan Rawlings, who wrote *The Yearling*.

Talent between the two? Probably the same. Level of education? Not much difference. But the Stranglers strangled, while the Wranglers were determined to give each other a life. The Stranglers promoted an atmosphere of contention and self-doubt. The Wranglers highlighted the best, not the worst.

Ted Engstrom

Of Mice and Maintenance Men

This is the place where I learned to live this life,
to curse this life and to claim this life for my very
own.

Jodie Foster

Over the past few weeks, I've loaded and unloaded
the dishwasher in my house a lot. One day, I filled and
emptied the darn thing on four separate occasions. Now,
for a mother with young, rambunctious children, so
many dishes in so little time probably wouldn't be out of
the ordinary. But I live with fifteen other women, all of
whom are relatively intelligent and mature Penn students, most of whom are at least twenty years old. So
why do the dishes—and the removal of the trash and
recycling, the sorting of the mail, the ordering of the
bottled water, the summoning of the exterminator and
the plumber, not to mention the disposal of the occasional mouse—all seem to fall to me?

Simple. I'm my sorority's house manager.

Last fall, my house was looking for a sister to manage

our property, in conjunction with our chapter accountant, an adult who keeps track of rent payments and makes sure the electricity stays on. The chapter wanted someone dependable—I wanted a single room. When my predecessor told me all I'd really have to do as house manager was remember to buy the toilet paper, I agreed to run for the job. I ran unopposed and was easily elected. My elation lasted about five seconds.

My problems started on move-in day, when I found the key box a jumble of mislabeled metal—and outright missing pieces. From there, we moved on to fortnightly visits from angry Penn police officers, summoned by our alarm company when someone left the house late and neglected to enter the code on the keypad before opening the door.

Shortly after, the pipe that supplies our two front bathrooms cracked in multiple places, spewing brown sludge onto the basement wall and carpet. Contractors then removed portions of the wall running up to the third floor and decided not to replace them until winter break, so as not to disturb our routine during midterms or finals. In retrospect, I wish I hadn't gotten such a close look at our home's infrastructure—which was more disturbing than any construction could have been.

Granted, these kinds of structural crises are likely to plague all buildings of a certain age at one time or another. Once I determined whom to call when something broke, I was fine.

There's no one to call, however, when two of your housemates are standing in the kitchen, staring at the wailing smoke detector on the ceiling, as if hoping that by sheer force of will *they will be able to make it stop!* (I suggested turning the stove off, or opening the back door to let air in, but they claimed that wouldn't allow them to cook their pasta.)

Then there was the time I walked in the front door, to be

met with a panic-stricken housemate running breathlessly up the basement stairs and screaming something about the washing machine flooding the laundry room. Fearlessly plunging my hand into the murky water in the sink where the machine empties, I discovered a sponge suctioned to the drain, stopping the flow of water. (Problem solved, except for the two inches of water on the floor, which I directed my housemate to take care of. Amazingly, she and a few others did.)

The most ridiculous incident occurred when we were temporarily out of powdered automatic-dishwasher detergent. Our supply company delivered powdered laundry soap by mistake. I was out of town, and one of my sisters signed for it, didn't bother reading the label, then ran the dishwasher through one cycle using it.

Another girl realized her mistake and tried to remedy the situation by putting liquid dishwashing soap—the kind you're supposed to use with rubber gloves in a sink full of water—into the automatic dishwasher. (If the result was a kitchen filled with suds, à la that famous episode of *The Brady Bunch* where the kids overload the washing machine, no one's yet had gumption enough to tell me.)

Given our gaffes, it's a wonder the house hasn't just collapsed. Seriously, though, as much as I complain about bagging trash, apologizing to and sending away the police and playing psychologist to unhappy roommates—activities my mom would have enthusiastically characterized as "learning experiences"—we haven't had any major catastrophes, and I'm thankful for that.

Still, after graduation—I'm renting.

Lisa Levenson

Knowing Where to Tap

Before setting off to college, my father sat me down and shared this memorable story with me. It is one I shall never forget. My father is not college educated, yet he possesses more wisdom and insight than most college professors I have met. After you read this story, you'll know what I mean.

There is an old story of a boilermaker who was hired to fix a huge steamship boiler system that was not working well. After listening to the engineer's description of the problems and asking a few questions, he went to the boiler room. He looked at the maze of twisting pipes, listened to the thump of the boiler and the hiss of escaping steam for a few minutes, and felt some pipes with his hands. Then he hummed softly to himself, reached into his overalls and took out a small hammer, and tapped a bright red valve one time. Immediately, the entire system began working perfectly, and the boilermaker went home. When the steamship owner received a bill for one thousand dollars, he complained that the boilermaker had only been in the engine room for fifteen minutes and requested an itemized bill. So the boilermaker sent him a bill that reads as follows:

For tapping the valve: $ .50

For knowing where to tap: $ 999.50

TOTAL: $1,000.00

"Tony," he said, "I want you to go to college so that you can get your degree, but more important, I want you to return with an education."

Tony D'Angelo

Miracle on Times Square

Broadway. The Great White Way. I was there—as an inventory clerk.

I was working my way through college, at Bond's Clothing Store on Times Square.

I had come to the United States from Tel Aviv, six thousand miles away, to study journalism. Walter Winchell was my idol. "Hello, Mr. and Mrs. America, and all the ships at sea!"

I had seen them in the movies, the news guys with "press" signs tucked into their hats. *The Front Page. His Girl Friday.* Being where exciting things were happening. Rushing into a phone booth, yelling, "Give me the city desk," into the receiver, then shouting, "Stop the presses!"

That was my dream. And here I was in America, twenty years old, living my dream. My parents, whose only child I was, had stayed behind in what was then Palestine, which I had left just months before the state of Israel was created. They had agreed to send me a hundred dollars a month, which back then, in 1948, was perhaps like a thousand today. But with the proclamation of the new nation, all permits for the transfer of money out of the country were canceled.

In other words, I could no longer count on help from home.

The job at Bond's, where I worked thirty hours a week, paid my bills. Long Island University in Brooklyn, where I was a sophomore, agreed to lower my tuition to a mere hundred dollars a semester. To make extra money, I worked as a doorman and usher at the Criterion Theater, a movie house underneath Bond's, during summer vacations. Dressed in a wine-colored uniform with shiny brass buttons, I stood at the theater entrance proclaiming, "Immediate seating in all parts of the theater! No waiting for seats!" I saw *Abbott and Costello in the Foreign Legion* forty times.

I did well in school, despite the fact that English was a foreign language to me. I had a steady girlfriend, Dalia, also from Tel Aviv. I lived in a furnished room in the Upper West Side, near her. I was self-supporting. I was living in America. Life was good.

And then, disaster struck.

On a warm summer evening, having collected my pay for the week at Bond's and at the Criterion, I took the subway home. Earlier in the day I had cashed the two paychecks and stuffed the bills into my wallet. After letting myself into my room, on Ninety-First Street near Broadway, I wanted to put my wallet away for the night. I put my hand in my left rear pocket. Nothing. Frantically I checked my other pockets. Still no wallet.

In the darkness of the theater, or perhaps on the subway, someone had deftly lifted my wallet, with all my money in it. All the money I had in the world. I sat on my bed, my head in my hands. Like most working college students, I lived from paycheck to paycheck. I had no bank account because I had no money to deposit. Damn! How cruel could people be? To steal a wallet from a working kid! Until that evening, I had only known the good side of people. My parents were kind and loving. In the ladies' department at Bond's, where I worked, I was "the kid from Israel" among the salespeople, all of them women. They mothered me and looked after me. At Long Island University, the dean of students had arranged my special tuition. And now I had been the victim of a crime.

The following morning I woke up with a headache, a sore throat and a 102-degree fever. My God! If I called in sick and didn't work, I wouldn't get paid! I was a part-time employee, with no benefits. And yet, if I went to work, I could become sicker. What to do?

I telephoned my doctor, who shortly thereafter examined me. "You've got the flu," he said. "Go home." I did. Then I called in sick.

I lay alone in my furnished room. I had no money, nor was I earning any. I was all alone in a foreign land. I was sick. I was twenty years old. I wanted to cry. But I heard my father's voice: "Men don't cry." So I didn't. I was sick for two weeks, during which Dalia's mother came daily with chicken soup. Dalia kept me company.

On a bright Monday morning, I staggered from the subway stop on Times Square to the store. I felt wiped out. Through the revolving door, past the men's accessories department, I nearly fell against Mr. Kissin, the manager. "Good to see you, my boy," he said. Rising slowly up the escalator, I saw my boss, Mrs. Menscher, waving to me, smiling a welcome.

"Sit, sit," she said. "Take a load off your feet. You look terrible."

Suddenly they were all around me: Miss Romano, the assistant manager, Mr. Price, from men's suits. Even Mr. Cooper, the district manager, came over.

"We have something for you," Mrs. Menscher said. She handed me an envelope. "Go on, open it."

I did. It was full of money.

"We took up a collection," she said. "It's a hundred dollars."

Tears filled my eyes. There was nothing to say but "Thanks, thanks. I'll never forget you."

And I haven't.

Dalia and I have been married more than forty-six years. We have three children and five grandchildren. I did become a reporter on major city newspapers.

The ups and downs of life have left me battered and bruised at times. The twentieth century has been the bloodiest example of man's inhumanity to man. Bond's is long gone, as are the people who worked there some fifty years ago. Dead they are, or ancient. And yet I learned an important lesson from them.

Perhaps Anne Frank said it best: "Despite everything, I still believe in the goodness of man."

Gunter David

The Dark Gift

The look on her face was one of numb disbelief. "It can't be," she says. "Why me? Why now?"

"It's not as bad as you're making it out to be," I said to my good friend Alex, as she sat there staring vacantly at the heavy cast on her leg. One moment she was running about, preparing for college, worrying about books, her car and which classes to take. Now, she was sitting here with a broken ankle. It all happened so suddenly.

This was the first time Alex had collided with an indifferent world. Everything else had been negotiable, arguable. Everything else up to now could be avoided, escaped, bought off, laughed away.

I tried to comfort her and tell her it would be all right. But this was real; this was hers. No one could change it, make it right, make it fair. It was life—an absolute without explanation—that was indifferent to her plans and dreams.

"My life is ruined," she sighed, feeling utterly depressed.

"No, your life isn't ruined. Just consider this one of those dark gifts. A bad circumstance can teach you something valuable, maybe even change your life."

Suddenly, I remembered the time several years ago when I, too, had broken an ankle. It was March. The streets were slushy paths, and corners were precarious hard-packed trails, through mounds of ice and snow. I struggled on crutches, trying to balance on uneven surfaces of ice. People pushed past me, muttering about how they had to get through, about how I was taking so long. I tried gingerly to make my way up over the snowpack without slipping or letting my cast drag in the slush. My arms ached from the tension, my shoulders were rigid and numb from the digging pain of the crutches. I tried to block out the others around me, not to feel them brushing brusquely past me.

Crutch by crutch, I made my way down to the street. Cars flew by, splashing slush on my cast. I hobbled into the street. The approaching cars were not slowing. I tried to hurry, but the icy ground was too precarious. Cars slid to a stop, and drivers leaned on their horns. I was consumed with my own fragile balance, ashamed of my deliberate pace, frustrated at others' lack of concern.

I looked across at the snowbank I would have to negotiate on the opposite side of the street. There, making her way down through the small uneven pathway of ice, was an old woman with a cane. People were standing behind her muttering. She was feeling with her foot, trying to find solid ground. No one could help her; there was not enough room for two abreast. I saw her frantic look, her shaking hands. Then, for an instant, she looked up. Across the distance of that icy, slush-filled street, our eyes met. The fear, the sadness, the frustration, the utter aloneness of our respective plights, were mirrored in our respective gazes.

I wanted to help her, but I could not. I could barely make my way across the street myself. The other pedestrians rushing past us were no help either. To them we were impediments to the necessary pace of daily living. To the drivers in the long line of cars that was backing up in the street, we were insufferable obstructions. We approached each other from opposite directions. As we passed, we glanced at each other.

"Hi," I said, not knowing what else to say.

She, who had the added fear of being elderly and alone on a city street, did not know whether to answer. Finally, she said, very softly, "Hello." Cars honked at the further slowing of pace that had been caused by our brief conversation. Other walkers brushed against us in their rush to get to the other side.

We looked again at each other, then went on. The cars revved and drove past in anger as soon as we were out of their path.

When I got to the other side, I turned to see how the woman was doing. She was feeling for the path through the snow with her cane. When she found her footing, she stopped as if she had accomplished a huge feat. She turned to look at me, and she smiled a sweet and tender smile. She knew I understood. For a moment she didn't feel so alone, and neither did I.

I wanted to tell Alex this story. But she was lost in her own world. I watched her as she put her backpack on and moved on unsteady crutches down the hallway. She had an evening class that she had to attend. "I never knew that doorknobs could be so much work," she said as she balanced on one leg and tried to open the door.

"Steps, revolving doors, taking baths, crossing streets. You've got a lot of fun ahead of you," I said. "But make sure to keep your eyes open for those dark gifts. They will be some of the best lessons you will ever be fortunate enough to learn."

Her pack slipped off her shoulder and almost pulled her over. I wanted to help her. But there was nothing I could do. "I'll never make fun of old people again," she said.

With that, I remembered the sweet smile of that woman. "Neither will I."

Kent Nerburn

Reverse Living

Life is tough.
It takes up a lot of your time, all your weekends,
and what do you get at the end of it?
. . . Death, a great reward.
I think the life cycle is all backwards.
You should die first, get it out of the way.
Then you should live twenty years in an old-age home.
You get kicked out when you're too young,
you get a gold watch, you go to work.
You work for forty years until you're
young enough to enjoy your retirement.
You go to college, you party until you're ready for high
    school,
you become a little kid, you play, you have no
    responsibilities,
you become a little boy or girl, you go back into the womb,
you spend your last nine months floating.
And you finish off as a gleam in someone's eye.

Norman Glass
Submitted by Tony D'Angelo

Blameless

I was a freshman in college when I met the Whites. They were completely different from my own family, yet I felt at home with them instantly. Jane White and I became friends at school, and her family welcomed me, an outsider, like a long-lost cousin.

In my family, when anything bad happened, it was always important to place blame.

"Who did this?" my mother would yell about a mess in the kitchen.

"This is all your fault, Katharine," my father would insist when the cat got out or the dishwasher broke.

From the time we were little, my sister and brothers and I told on each other. We set a place for Blame at the dinner table.

But the Whites didn't worry about who had done what. They picked up the pieces and moved on with their lives. The beauty of this was driven home to me the summer that Jane died.

Mr. and Mrs. White had six children: three sons and three daughters. One son had passed away in childhood, which may be why the surviving five siblings remained so close.

In July, the White sisters and I decided to take a car trip from their home in Florida to New York. The two oldest, Sarah and Jane, were college students, and the youngest, Amy, had recently turned sixteen. The proud possessor of a brand-new driver's license, Amy was excited about practicing her driving on the trip. With her endearing giggle, she showed off her license to everyone she met.

The big sisters shared the driving of Sarah's new car during the first part of the trip, but when they reached less populated areas, they let Amy take over. Somewhere in South Carolina, we pulled off the highway to eat. After lunch, Amy got behind the wheel. She came to an intersection with a stop sign for her direction only. Whether she was flustered or distracted or just didn't see the sign no one will ever know, but Amy continued into the intersection without stopping. The driver of a large semi-tractor-trailer, unable to brake in time, plowed into our vehicle.

Jane was killed instantly.

I survived the accident with only a few bruises. The most difficult thing that I've ever done was to call the Whites to tell them about the accident and that Jane had died. As painful as it was for me to lose a good friend, I knew that it was far worse for them to lose a child.

When Mr. and Mrs. White arrived at the hospital, they found their two surviving daughters sharing a room. Sarah's head was wrapped in bandages; Amy's leg was in a cast. They hugged us all and cried tears of sadness and of joy at seeing their daughters. They wiped away the girls' tears and teased a few giggles out of Amy as she learned to use her crutches.

To both of their daughters, and especially to Amy, over and over they simply said, "We're so glad that you're alive."

I was astonished. No accusations. No blame.

Later, I asked the Whites why they never talked about

the fact that Amy was driving and had run a stop sign.

Mrs. White said, "Jane's gone, and we miss her terribly. Nothing we say or do will bring her back. But Amy has her whole life ahead of her. How can she lead a full and happy life if she feels we blame her for her sister's death?"

They were right. Amy graduated from college and got married several years ago. She works as a teacher of learning-disabled students. She's also a mother of two little girls of her own, the oldest named Jane.

I learned from the Whites that blame really isn't very important. Sometimes, there's no use for it at all.

Kathy Johnson Gale

5

LOVE 101

A chemist who can extract from his heart's element, compassion, respect, longing, patience, regret, surprise and forgiveness and compound them into one can create that atom which is called love.

Kahlil Gibran

Finding My Way

I started college when I was sixteen years old. It was a big, scary place, and I was young. I remember standing in line for registration with the hordes of other people. I felt so insecure and inadequate next to those who were my supposed peers. *How would I ever measure up to these people who seemed so confident and sure of what they wanted?*

I didn't have any specific direction. I didn't have a clue as to what I wanted to do or be. College was just the next logical step. I felt very much out of place. To me, these people around me embodied my picture of the consummate college student. They stood there laughing with their friends, a cup of coffee in one hand, the schedule of classes in the other, discussing their options for the upcoming semester. Me, I had a list of classes on a piece of paper that I had painstakingly worked out with my big brother the night before. If I didn't get those particular classes, I was sunk. The idea of having a backup plan never even occurred to me. What would I do? I would just die. I knew that crying wasn't an option—I was in college for heaven's sake! Maybe throwing up would be a more socially acceptable reaction. I was alone, nervous and feeling like a cartoon in a museum of priceless paintings.

When the first week of classes started, I had the daunting task of trying to figure out where my classes were in
this city they called a school. I was already exhausted by
the overwhelming task of trying to park my car. Feeling
awkward, out of place and in a world of logistical nightmares, studying and getting an education were the last
things on my mind. But I put one foot in front of the
other and prayed I would find some solace somewhere.
And I did.

He walked into my life and into the huge auditorium
that looked more like a movie theater than a classroom.
But instead of taking a seat in the large lecture hall, he
continued toward the front of the room to teach the class.
He was smart and funny. I started to find any excuse to
visit his office. This strange new world started to hold
new meaning for me, and I began to explore it with more
bravado. That was the good news. The bad news was that
I had a crush on a man who was twice my age, married
and had a family. But I felt helpless among all these new
feelings and experiences I was having. Was this what
becoming an adult meant? It all seemed too confusing.

I excelled in his class. One day he asked me if I wanted
to help him grade papers, file and do some office work—a
teacher's aide of sorts. There was no need to ask me twice.
As the weeks passed, we shared lots of time together. I
learned how to drink coffee over long philosophical conversations. We became friends.

Much to my surprise, out of the blue, he asked me if I
would consider doing some baby-sitting for him. I was
getting an invitation to become part of his private world.
I was given directions to his house and told to come by
that Thursday.

I arrived at his house promptly at six. He greeted me at
the door. "Thank you so much for doing this. It's very
important to me." He explained that his wife was taking

care of her ailing mother and had taken their eight-month-old baby with her. Lily, their six-year-old, needed special care, and he was hoping to find someone who would click with her.

"Lily has cystic fibrosis and spends too much of her little life in bed." My heart just broke as I saw the love he had in his eyes for his little girl.

He took me into her room and, in the middle of a princess bed, sat this fair-haired little angel. She had some sort of breathing apparatus next to her bed that looked strangely out of place. What happened next was something I wasn't prepared for.

"This is the girl I told you about, Sweetie," he signed to his daughter. It turned out that Lily was deaf as well. I panicked. How would I communicate with her? What if there was an emergency?

"Her oral skills are good enough that you will be able to understand her, and you'll probably pick up some sign language. I'll only be gone a couple of hours." He left me with emergency numbers and pertinent information, and then he was gone.

I sat down on the bed with Lily, and her little fingers started flying. I shrugged my shoulders to let her know that I was lost. She smiled sweetly and then started to use her voice. She explained how it was easier to breathe when she let her fingers do her talking. That night I had my first lesson in sign language.

Over the next couple of months, I spent a lot of time with Lily. As I got to know Lily's dad as a father and as a husband, the crush changed. Now I was falling in love with his daughter. She taught me so much: not only how to sign, but also how to appreciate each moment in my life and how worrying over needless things was just stupid. We laughed together when she taught me the sign for stupid, where you take the closed fist of your right hand and knock on the side of your forehead—as if you're knocking to try to get in. She laughed as I made believe that I was hurting myself by knocking on my head too hard. And she would sign, "You hurt yourself just as much when you really do worry." She was wise beyond her years. Besides giving me her love, Lily also gave me direction. I went on to get a bachelor's degree in special education with an emphasis in deaf education.

I remained friends with Lily and her whole family throughout my college years and beyond. The crush I had on my college professor served me very well. I learned a great deal about life at the hands of a young child.

Some years later, I was asked to sign the Lord's Prayer at Lily's funeral. Everyone there told stories about how this one small life made such a big difference to so many. And, as Lily taught me when she showed me the sign for *I love you*, "Make sure when you use this sign that you really mean it."

Zan Gaudioso

The Mirror

Her name was Jillene Jones. Jillene Jones! The alliteration just added to her mystique. To me, she was a character in the great American novel; the star of a blockbuster movie; the president of my world. She was truly the woman for me. I just knew it. Now if I could only find out something about her.

I asked around. I was Jim Rockford, Sherlock Holmes and Magnum P.I. all rolled into one. First clue: She was into heavy metal. Cool! Well, not so cool. Actually, I couldn't stand heavy metal. My hearing's a little sensitive, especially when the noise level exceeds that of a cannon blast. So what—who needs to hear? A lot of unwanted noise in this world anyway. I started listening to heavy metal.

Second clue: She liked to work out. I joined her gym. The machines in there looked like they were designed for some sort of bizarre psychological testing. Since there didn't appear to be any instruction manuals, I decided to stick to something simple like the treadmill. What fun! What a high! Actually, I felt like a hamster in a wheel. No matter. I was moving closer to my goal.

I decided to make some discreet inquiries among her

friends. The fates were truly on my side because not only did the woman of my dreams, Jillene Jones, know who I was, but she didn't find me totally repulsive. The die was cast. The plot was set. She would be mine. Even though the die was cast and the plot was set, etc., it took me another week to get up the courage to ask her out.

More research. Third clue: She loved Aramis. What an amazing coincidence! I loved Aramis, too—until I smelled it. Yikes. But surely if Jillene Jones loved Aramis, it must be an acquired taste. I bought the econo-size bottle of Aramis and began wearing it every day, everywhere I went. Every time I smelled my unique odor, I thought of Jillene Jones. And strangely enough, I began to notice a change in the way others perceived me. I always found a seat on the bus. If I had to stand in line, people would step aside and let me move to the front. Animals and small children fled in fear as I walked down the street. No matter, because I was on a quest.

A little more research and I would be ready. Clues four, five and six: She loved the color peach, bowling and sushi. I bought a peach-colored bowling shirt, found a bowling alley that served sushi and learned to throw strikes. Finally, I got up my courage and made the call. Luck was in my favor; the most popular head-banging band around was playing at our local college venue. I finagled great seats after draining my meager bank account. I put on my best Barry White baritone (which sounded more like Steve Urkel on a bad day) and asked Jillene Jones out on a date. She said yes.

The stars were aligned. All was right with the world. I saw my destiny and it had a name: Jillene Jones. The day of what would surely be the best night of my life began at the gym. Forty-five minutes on the hamster mill. I saw her out of the corner of my eye. Did she notice my Motley Crue T-shirt? I could only hope. The night finally arrived.

I put on my peach bowling shirt, drenched myself in Aramis, spiked my hair and threw in a fake nose ring for good measure.

Her eyes lit up when she saw that peach bowling shirt. "You know I was watching you today," she said. "You looked pretty cute on that treadmill. I didn't know you were a metal-head!" She saw the shirt!!! My plan was working!!! I walked her to my car and popped in a little Ozzy. She didn't seem to notice that the volume blew out all four of my speakers. She just grooved to the buzzing.

We went to the concert and I screamed at her for three hours until my ears felt like they were bleeding. Then mercifully the band finally stopped and we were able to leave. Sushi. She ordered some really slimy, expensive stuff that slid down my throat like dead goldfish. I had to pretend to use the restroom and sneak out to my car to gather all the spare change from the floorboards to pay the bill.

I drove her home and walked her to the door. She gave me a kiss that should be reserved for sailors going to sea. I had won her over. She was mine!!! Then she said the six words that I had never imagined, in my wildest fantasies, hearing: "Would you like to come in?"

Before my rational mind could answer, something came out from some part of my being that I heretofore did not know existed. "No," I said. I looked around, wondering where that had come from. She looked at me in disbelief and said good night.

I drove myself home in silence. Well, I really had no choice since my speakers were blown. I walked inside and went into the bathroom. I looked at myself in the mirror. There I was with spiky hair, a fake nose ring and wearing a peach bowling shirt. I reeked of dead fish and cheap cologne. My ears were ringing so loud I kept picking up the phone. Who was I? Jillene Jones. I remembered some

National Geographic special I had once seen on TV where the narrator described how lions hunt. "They become their prey." But starting a relationship shouldn't be a hunt. That didn't seem right.

I took off the peach bowling shirt and the nose ring. I rinsed out my hair and put on some mellow jazz. I went back into the bathroom and looked again in the mirror. There I was. Me. And somewhere out there was a woman for ME.

Every once in a while I pass an Aramis counter in a department store or smell someone wearing that potent scent and I think of Jillene Jones. The name still rolls off my tongue. I wish her well and hope she found that special peach-shirt-wearing, sushi-loving, treadmill-running, Aramis-drenched, bowling metal-head to love.

Dan Clark

I Dare You!

On the first day of my second year at California State University at Sacramento, I saw the most gorgeous guy! He was standing alone in line at the cafeteria and looked out of place. Turning to my friends, I said, "I have to meet him!"

Challenging my spontaneity, my friends reached into their purses and came up with money for a bet. They then dared me to run up to him, pretend that I knew him and convince him that he knew me. Smiling, I turned and was off to meet the cutie pie.

"Dan, Dan!" I yelled as I ran up to him. "How are you? How's your mom?" He just stood there looking at me. I could tell that he was shy. I liked him immediately.

"I'm not Dan," he said, looking a little confused.

"Sure you are!" I countered. "You lived in Sierra Hall last year, third floor! You were Bob's roommate."

"No, I lived off campus last year," this sweet man replied, still not getting it. I turned and started to leave, and he began asking me a series of questions: "Do I know you from my mom's allergy clinic?" (I hate shots.) "Were you in the parrot class I took last summer?" (I like birds only slightly more than shots.) "Do you eat at Taco Bell? I work there." (Never.)

"Well," he said, "I know I'm not Dan, and I didn't live in Sierra Hall." He reached out his hand to mine. "My name is Tim, and I'm pleased to meet you anyway."

He invited me to his fraternity party that night. I composed myself and informed him that I did not go to fraternity parties. But as I watched him walk away, I had second thoughts. That afternoon, I took the money that I'd won from the bet and bought a black miniskirt. I was going to my first fraternity party.

When I arrived there, I was a little nervous. Would he be there? When I got to the front steps of the frat house, I looked up and saw Tim sitting at the top. He looked at me and smiled.

"I was hoping you would come. I've been waiting for you." I sat down next to him and we started talking. We talked all that night—and for the next three nights—until dawn. Four months later, he asked me to marry him. Four years later, we tied the knot. This year, we celebrated the fifteenth anniversary of the day we met.

Some nights when we are snuggling together, I'm reminded that I found my soul mate on a dare. Now and then, my husband asks, "Am I Dan or Tim tonight?" Having a special place in my heart for both of them, I always laugh and reply, "You decide!"

April Kemp

The Love I'll Never Forget

The moment you have in your heart this extraordinary thing called love and feel the depth, the delight, the ecstasy of it, you will discover that the world is transformed.

J. Krishnamurti

My Minnesota hometown is a farming community of eight thousand people, tucked into the northwest corner of the state. Not a lot that is extraordinary passes through. Gretchen was an exception.

Gretchen was an Eickhof, a member of one of the town's wealthiest families. They lived in a sprawling brick place on the banks of the Red Lake River and spent summers at their vacation home on Union Lake, thirty miles away.

But there was nothing snooty about Gretchen. In sixth grade, she broke both legs skiing and for months had to be carried around by her father. After that, she taught herself to walk again. In high school, she tutored students less able than herself and was among the first to befriend new kids at school. Years later, she told me she had also been the "guardian angel" who left cookies and inspirational notes at my locker before my hockey games. She moved through the various elements of high-school society—farm kids, jocks and geeks—dispensing goodwill to all. Gretchen, the Central High Homecoming Queen of 1975, was clearly going places.

I knew her only well enough to exchange greetings when we passed in the halls. I was a good athlete and, in the parlance of the time, kind of cute. But I was insecure, especially around females. Girls were mysterious creatures, more intimidating than fastballs hurled high and tight, which may explain my bewilderment one midsummer night in 1977 when I bumped into Gretchen at a local hangout. I had just finished my freshman year at the University of North Dakota in nearby Grand Forks. Gretchen, whose horizons were much broader, was home from California after her first year at Stanford.

She greeted me happily. I remember the feel of her hand, rough as leather from hours in the waters of Union Lake, as she pulled me toward the dance floor. She was nearly as tall as I, with perfect almond skin, soft features and almost fluorescent white teeth. Honey-blond hair hung in strands past her shoulders. Her sleeveless white shirt glowed in the strobe lights, setting off arms that were brown and strong from swimming, horseback riding and canoeing.

Though not much of a dancer, Gretchen moved to the music enthusiastically, smiling dreamily. After a few dances we stood and talked, yelling to each other over the music. By the time I walked her to her car, Main Street was deserted. The traffic light blinked yellow. We held hands as we walked. When we arrived at her car, she invited me to kiss her. I was glad to oblige.

But where hometown boys were concerned, Gretchen was as elusive as mercury. As passionately as she returned some of my kisses that summer and the next, for her, I was part of the interlude between childhood and the more serious endeavors to come. I, however, was dizzy for her and had the bad habit of saying so. Each time I did, she pulled away from me. These were college summers, not the time for moony eyes and vows of undying devotion.

One night in 1978 when Gretchen and I were together, out of nowhere she spoke the words that guys in my situation dread above all.

"Tim," she said, "I think we should just be friends."

I told her I was tired of her games and was not as much of a fool as she thought. I stormed away. By morning, I had cooled off. I sent her some roses that day, with a note offering an apology and my friendship.

Gretchen and I started dating again about a month later. But this time I had learned my lesson. No more moony eyes. I could be as detached and aloof as the next guy. It worked beautifully, except that after a few weeks Gretchen asked, "What's wrong with you?"

"What do you mean, what's wrong?"

"You're not yourself," she said. "You haven't been for a long time."

"I know," I said, and let her in on my ruse. For the only time I remember, she became angry. Then she proposed a deal.

"You be who you are," she said, "and I won't go anywhere, at least for the rest of the summer."

It was a bargain I quickly accepted. She was as good as her word.

Those weeks seemed golden, a bit unreal. One time as we said good night, I discarded the final wisp of my caution and told Gretchen that I loved her. She only smiled.

I came back from college to see her off to Stanford in mid-September. While Gretchen packed, I absently shot pool at her father's table. When she finished, we took a last walk around her family's horse pasture in the gathering September chill. I thought how dramatically our lives were about to diverge and was saddened. But more than anything, I was thankful for the fine, fun times we had spent over the last two summers.

Gretchen planned to find work in California next summer. For her, the serious part of life beckoned, and I knew what that meant.

"Good-bye," I said as we stood at her front door.

"Don't say 'good-bye,'" she replied. "Say 'see you later.'"

A month later, the last of the autumn leaves were falling, but the sky was a cloudless blue, the air crisp and invigorating. Classes were done for the day.

The telephone rang the second I stepped into my dorm room. I recognized Gretchen's friend Julie's voice on the other end of the line, and my heart soared. Julie was to be married the following month, and maybe Gretchen would be returning home for the wedding after all. But hearing the uncharacteristically quiet scratch of Julie's voice, I knew before she told me that Gretchen was dead.

The previous morning Gretchen had collected one of her birthday presents from a college friend: a ride in a small plane. Shortly after takeoff, the craft lurched out of control and pitched into a marsh. Gretchen and her friend were killed instantly.

"Gretchen's parents wondered if you would be a pallbearer," Julie said.

"I'd be honored," I heard myself reply. The word sounded strange even as it left my mouth. *Honored?* Is that what I felt?

I left my dormitory and walked aimlessly. I am told I sought out a campus priest, but eighteen years later I have no memory of that. *How does a person grieve?* I wondered, unable to cry.

The night after the funeral, I sat with my high-school buddy Joel in his Chevy Vega outside the restaurant where Gretchen's mourning friends planned to congregate.

Seeing him was the beginning of both my pain and my consolation, for as Joel spoke of Gretchen, his voice briefly failed. That tiny catch in my old friend's voice dissolved whatever stood between my sorrow and me. My torrents of grief were unleashed.

The next morning, Joel and I joined a procession from the Eickhofs' lakeside summer house into the nearby woods. Gretchen's sisters took turns carrying a small urn that contained her ashes. It was cool and sunny, and the fallen leaves crackled underfoot.

We came to a lone birch tree, its magnificent white bark standing out among the surrounding maples. Scratched into the trunk were the names of Gretchen, her father and her younger sister, as well as a date many years before.

Someone said a prayer. Gretchen's father placed the urn in the ground below the birch. Above us, wind rustled through newly barren branches.

I was among the last to leave. I emerged from the woods that day into a different world, where memories of first love linger but summers always end.

Tim Madigan

Heartbreak 101

I like to think of myself as a real risk taker. Just yesterday, I crossed the street when the *Don't Walk* sign had already begun flashing. The day before that, I ate dessert before dinner. You might say I live on the edge.

Well, actually, you probably wouldn't say that.

My mom tells me I started walking when I was eleven months old—and then changed my mind and decided to go back to crawling for a few more months. Too many chances of falling when you're on two legs, I guess. In high school, my friend Jill (a girl who pierced her belly button before anyone else) tried to teach me to smoke behind the football field. I took one puff and threw up. True, it was gross, but mostly I think I puked because I felt guilty and scared of getting caught.

See, I'm chicken. And until I got to college, I'd always maintained that being chicken worked in my favor. I was in control. By playing it safe, nothing really bad ever happened to me.

But by the time my parents left me in my dorm room at the University of Wisconsin, I was ready to say goodbye to them and to the old me. It was time to start living fear free. This was the first time I'd ever really left home.

I decided that when opportunities arose, instead of crawling under my covers, I'd be wide awake for them. I was going to loosen the white-knuckle grip I had on my life and start taking risks.

Starring in my new role as The Girl Who Takes Chances, I decided I would have to get used to making the first move. So I approached the funky girl in the zoology lab with purple hair and glitter eyeliner and asked to be her partner. Soon thereafter, she became my best friend. Instead of studying together, Liz and I held late-night séances to contact the spirit of our zoology professor. He wasn't dead, of course; we just thought maybe his unconscious would give us the test answers. On Saturday afternoons, we would take a bus to a town we'd never been to and wander around, exploring thrift shops and discussing what we had in common. We each had a brother named Steve; we both hated coconut.

My friendship with Liz gave me confidence that—in my previous life—would have made me squirm. I joined the campus hiking club, which may not seem particularly daring, but I'd never done anything like it before. It wasn't tightrope walking, I told myself, but it did pose a few dangers: unexpected thunderstorms, getting lost in the woods, mosquitoes. It was something new and a little bit scary (like having to wear ankle-high hiking boots in case I stepped on a snake), but I was brave.

However, it wasn't until I walked right up to a cute guy and introduced myself that I realized I had practically become a different person. Well, not exactly. I was just doing my homework. On the first day of Psych 101, the professor told us to do something we'd never done before. So I went to a local coffee shop and asked the finest guy there if I could join him.

"It's an assignment," I said, smiling, as I slipped my insanely clammy hands into my pockets.

He looked at me like I was crazy, and then he laughed and pulled out the chair next to him. David turned out to be smart and funny—a philosophy major who also watched *Party of Five*. We ended up talking until the coffee shop closed.

If that were the end of the story, then the moral would be simple: Take risks, seek new experiences, meet awesome friends and a hot guy, be happy, the end. Except, as I learned in my freshman creative-writing class, a good story never ends where you think it will.

The day after we met at the coffee shop, David called and invited me to do laundry with him. At first, I couldn't decide if this was cool and quirky or just a pathetic excuse for a date. (And yes, the idea of debuting my underwear totally freaked me out.) But somewhere around the spin cycle, I got hooked. Here was a guy who knew his knits from his delicates and wasn't afraid to admit it.

After that, the Laundromat was a regular event. He and Liz got along great, too. I'd introduced them in October, and by Thanksgiving, the three of us were hanging out together regularly—pulling all-nighters at the Denny's near my dorm, even making plans to get our heads shaved together. (David was the only one who actually did it.)

One night in early winter when I had too much studying to do, David and Liz went to an Ani DiFranco concert. A few days later, David couldn't stop talking about how cool Liz was. "We had the best time!" he raved.

"Should I start worrying about leaving you two alone?" I asked.

"That's sick, Lauren," he answered quickly. "You're a real sicko."

But two days after Christmas, David dumped me. By New Year's Eve, he and Liz were an item, ringing in their romance at a Thai restaurant near campus that David and I had discovered. I was immobilized on my parents' sofa back in Milwaukee with Dick Clark, a bowl of popcorn and a king-size box of tissues to keep me company. I was even wearing David's University of Chicago sweatshirt because it still smelled like him.

I'd become daring, and suddenly life hurt worse than I could believe.

I was miserable. It was my fault, I thought, for getting close to new people so quickly. For my best efforts, as I saw it, I'd been betrayed, rejected and doubly dumped. These were not things that happened to me in high school. These were not things that happened to mature college students who were in control of their lives.

I seriously thought about transferring. And then, after several weeks of moping in my dorm and many, many Hostess cupcakes, I thought about something else: Brave people don't limp off to another school after they've been wounded in battle. They grab their swords (and their cupcakes) and move on.

So I took a deep breath and went to the next hiking-club meeting. I started on some new stories for my creative-writing class: tragic tales about girls whose hearts were torn out of their chests and squashed like bugs or— depending on my mood—who wreaked gory revenge on people who'd betrayed them (but still, they were stories all the same). And, eventually, I gathered up my courage and told David and Liz how they had temporarily destroyed me. It was ugly. But I did it.

Okay, so I don't rush out to sign up for skydiving classes, and I can't bring myself to even read about death-defying climbs up Mount Everest. But the fact is, unexpected things happen to you no matter how safe (or boring) you try to be. Dealing with them on your own and persevering is what college—and life—is about. Now I realize that learning to bounce back from a bad experience was more valuable than any A I've ever earned.

Lauren Fox

What Is Sex?

One day in an emergency waiting room, a little girl turned to her mother and asked, "What is sex?" People turned their full attention to Mom. I mean, this was better than whatever was on the waiting-room television—better than *Jerry Springer.* I mean this was real life. Exciting. What was Mom going to say? How do you answer a six-year-old girl? What is sex? This is one hot topic. You know, kids seem to know so much more than I did at their age; they are exposed to so much more these days on television and at the movies. How was Mom going to answer?

I'm the kind of guy who just goes ahead and answers the question right away, like I not only know the answer, but understand the question. So I'm curious how Mom is going to tell this little girl about how babies are made. Or how Mom is going to dodge this difficult question. I mean, is Mom going to talk to a little child about safe sex? I'm pretty sure Mom is not going to talk about ways to have sex; although you just really never know what might happen in the emergency room.

But she surprises me; she doesn't think in the way I think or respond the way I usually respond. Instead, she pauses. I hardly ever pause. She then thoughtfully asks her daughter, "What do you mean, dear?" The little girl responds, "Well, Mom, I was looking at this paper, and it says sex—M/F. Am I an M or an F?" Mom's face breaks into a huge smile. The waiting room patrons resume their usual chatter.

And I laugh. I would have answered the wrong question. I had heard the question, but I really did not listen to what the little girl was saying.

Adam Saperston
Submitted by Kathleen Kelly

Swans Mate for Life

The end of my sophomore year was approaching. Mom called me at the dorm one muggy evening during the last week of May. My summer break would be spent with Grandma and Grandpa, helping out around their farm. The arrangement made good sense to all the family. I wasn't fully convinced of that myself but figured it was just one summer. Next year would be my little brother's turn.

I packed my car after my last exam and said my good-byes until the fall. My friends would keep until then. Most of them were going home for the summer anyway.

The farm was about a three-hour drive from school. My grandparents were both in their seventies, and I knew they really needed the help around the farm. Getting in the hay would be something Grandpa couldn't do by himself. He also needed help with repairs to the barns and a host of other chores.

I arrived late that afternoon. Grandma had fixed more food than the three of us could possibly eat. She doted over me entirely too much. I figured all the attention would taper off once she got used to having me around, but it didn't. Grandpa wanted to bring me up to date on literally everything. By the time I settled in for bed that night, I'd decided things would be okay. After all, it was just for one summer.

The next morning, Grandpa fixed breakfast for the two of us. He told me Grandma had tired herself out yesterday and was going to rest in bed a little longer. I made a mental note to myself to not ask her to do things for me while I was there. I was there to help, not be a burden.

Grandpa surprised me that morning. Once we were out of the house, he seemed more in his own element. The farm was his domain. Despite his age, there was confidence in the way he moved about the place. He didn't seem like the same person who had fallen asleep last night on the couch before the six o'clock news was finished. As we walked the pastures getting a close-up look at the livestock, Grandpa seemed to know each cow. And there were nearly two hundred of them!

We didn't do much real work that first day, but I gained a sense of appreciation for what Grandpa had done all those years before I was even born. He wasn't an educated man, but he had raised and provided for four children on this farm. I was impressed by that.

Weeks passed. By June we had already baled one cutting of hay and gotten it safely into the barn. I gradually settled into a routine of daily work with Grandpa. He had a mental schedule of things that needed doing, and we worked on part of it each day. In the evenings I usually read or talked with Grandma. She never grew tired of hearing about college or anything I was involved in. She told me stories about her childhood, family and the early years after she and Grandpa had married.

The last Saturday in June, Grandpa suggested we go fishing, since we were caught up on everything. The pond was in a low pasture near the woods. Years before, Grandpa had stocked it with fish. We drove the pickup to the pond that day, looking over the livestock as we went. We hadn't expected what we saw when we got to the pond that morning: One of the swans was dead. Grandpa had given the pair of swans to Grandma on their fiftieth anniversary.

"Why don't we see about buying another one," I suggested, hoping the situation could somehow be righted. Grandpa thought for a few moments before answering. He finally said, "No . . . it's not that easy, Bruce. You see, swans mate for life." He raised his finger to point, holding the fishing pole in his other hand. "There's nothing we can do for the one that's left. He has to work it out for himself."

We caught enough fish that morning for lunch. On the way back to the house, Grandpa asked me not to tell Grandma about the swan. She didn't get down to the pond much anymore, and there was no sense in her knowing about it right away.

A few days later, we drove by the pond while doing our morning check on the cows. We found the other swan lying near the same spot we had found the first one. It, too, was dead.

The month of July started with me and Grandpa putting up a new stretch of fence. Then July 12 came. That was the day Grandma passed away. I'd overslept that morning. Grandpa had not knocked on my door, either. It was nearly eight o'clock by the time I could hurriedly dress myself and get down to the kitchen. I saw Dr. Morgan sitting at the kitchen table. He was a neighbor my grandparents' age, long since retired. He'd come to the house several times before on social calls. I immediately knew something was wrong. This morning, his tattered old black bag was by his feet, and my grandfather was obviously shaken.

Grandma had died suddenly that morning of a stroke. By the afternoon, my parents were there. The old house was soon crowded with relatives and Grandpa's friends.

The funeral was held the next day. Grandpa had insisted on having it as soon as possible. On the second day after the funeral, Grandpa announced at the breakfast table, "This is a working farm. We have a lot of things to do. The rest of you should get back to your own lives." Most of the family had already left, but this was Grandpa's way of telling the rest it was time for them to go home. My parents were the last to leave after lunch.

Grandpa was not a man who could outwardly express his grief around others, and we all worried about him. There had been talk of his giving up the farm. My parents thought he was too old to live out there alone. He wouldn't hear of it, though. I was proud of the way the old man had stood his ground.

The rest of the summer flowed by. We stayed busy working. I thought there was something different about Grandpa but couldn't quite put my finger on it. I started to wonder if he would be better off living with someone after all, but I knew he could not leave the farm.

September was nearing, and part of me did not want to leave. I thought of skipping the fall semester and staying around a few more months. When I mentioned it, Grandpa quickly told me that my place was back at college.

The day finally came for me to pack my car and leave. I shook his hand and chanced a hug. As I drove down the driveway, I saw him in the rearview mirror. He waved to me and then walked to the pasture gate to start the morning livestock check. That's how I like to remember him.

Mom called me at school on a blustery October day to tell me Grandpa had died. A neighbor had stopped by that morning for coffee and found him in the kitchen. He died of a stroke, same as Grandma. At that moment, I understood what he'd clumsily tried to explain to me about the swan on that morning we fished together by the pond.

Hal Torrance

6

ACTS OF KINDNESS

*J*oin the great company of those who make the
barren places of life fruitful with kindness.

Helen Keller

The Boy Under the Tree

In the summer recess between freshman and sopho-more years in college, I was invited to be an instructor at a high-school leadership camp hosted by a college in Michigan. I was already highly involved in most campus activities, and I jumped at the opportunity.

About an hour into the first day of camp, amid the frenzy of icebreakers and forced interactions, I first noticed the boy under the tree. He was small and skinny, and his obvi-ous discomfort and shyness made him appear frail and fragile. Only fifty feet away, two hundred eager campers were bumping bodies, playing, joking and meeting each other, but the boy under the tree seemed to want to be anywhere other than where he was. The desperate loneli-ness he radiated almost stopped me from approaching him, but I remembered the instructions from the senior staff to stay alert for campers who might feel left out.

As I walked toward him, I said, "Hi, my name is Kevin, and I'm one of the counselors. It's nice to meet you. How are you?" In a shaky, sheepish voice he reluctantly answered, "Okay, I guess." I calmly asked him if he wanted to join the activities and meet some new people. He quietly replied, "No, this is not really my thing."

I could sense that he was in a new world, that this whole experience was foreign to him. But I somehow knew it wouldn't be right to push him, either. He didn't need a pep talk; he needed a friend. After several silent moments, my first interaction with the boy under the tree was over.

At lunch the next day, I found myself leading camp songs at the top of my lungs for two hundred of my new friends. The campers eagerly participated. My gaze wandered over the mass of noise and movement and was caught by the image of the boy from under the tree, sitting alone, staring out the window. I nearly forgot the words to the song I was supposed to be leading. At my first opportunity, I tried again, with the same questions as before: "How are you doing? Are you okay?" To which he again replied, "Yeah, I'm all right. I just don't really get into this stuff." As I left the cafeteria, I realized this was going to take more time and effort than I had thought—if it was even possible to get through to him at all.

That evening at our nightly staff meeting, I made my concerns about him known. I explained to my fellow staff members my impression of him and asked them to pay special attention and spend time with him when they could.

The days I spend at camp each year fly by faster than any others I have known. Thus, before I knew it, mid-week had dissolved into the final night of camp, and I was chaperoning the "last dance." The students were doing all they could to savor every last moment with their new "best friends"—friends they would probably never see again.

As I watched the campers share their parting moments, I suddenly saw what would be one of the most vivid memories of my life. The boy from under the tree, who had stared blankly out the kitchen window, was now a shirtless dancing wonder. He owned the dance floor as he and two girls proceeded to cut a rug. I watched as he shared meaningful, intimate time with people at whom he couldn't even look just days earlier. I couldn't believe it was the same person.

In October of my sophomore year, a late-night phone call pulled me away from my chemistry book. A soft-spoken, unfamiliar voice asked politely, "Is Kevin there?"

"You're talking to him. Who's this?"

"This is Tom Johnson's mom. Do you remember Tommy from leadership camp?"

The boy under the tree. How could I not remember?

"Yes, I do," I said. "He's a very nice young man. How is he?"

An abnormally long pause followed, then Mrs. Johnson said, "My Tommy was walking home from school this week when he was hit by a car and killed." Shocked, I offered my condolences.

"I just wanted to call you," she said, "because Tommy mentioned you so many times. I wanted you to know that he went back to school this fall with confidence. He made new friends. His grades went up. And he even went out on a few dates. I just wanted to thank you for making a difference for Tom. The last few months were the best few months of his life."

In that instant, I realized how easy it is to give a bit of yourself every day. You may never know how much each gesture may mean to someone else. I tell this story as often as I can, and when I do, I urge others to look out for their own "boy under the tree."

David Coleman and Kevin Randall

For the Kids

A little boy smiled as he played within an octopus of tubes and electrodes that measured his every breath and all his vital signs. He looked up and said, "My IV is out," sending a student scurrying down the hall to the nurse's station. A little girl in a room down the hall lay quiet in her bed. Her tiny bald head peered through the hospital rails at the visiting students. "I have cancer," she whispered. "I can spell it for you."

In addition to their illnesses, the children in this hospital had one more thing in common: the need for medical supplies and services that their insurance companies would not cover. That afternoon, a routine tour of the hospital for thirteen college students became a year-long project as we realized these kids needed more than our visits.

We called ourselves the "Dream Team." Working with Children's Miracle Network, we spent the next year planning a thirty-two-hour dance marathon that would raise the money. In the face of the courage and energy shown by these kids, no one could see thirty-two hours of nonstop dancing as too much of a task. We had no problem collecting over three hundred student volunteers to plan the event. "Thon" fever had exploded on the campus and in the community. Our goal was five thousand dollars, and we were sure we would meet it.

Each sorority, fraternity, residence hall and student organization "adopted" the family of a sick child. The families were embraced by the campus on almost monthly visits to football games, chapter meetings and dinners in the cafeteria. The students followed their child's health, wrote cards and made frequent trips to the hospital. The children were given love and the hope that they might be able to go to college themselves one day. Students stood at intersections in minus-forty-degree wind chill, collecting spare change. Faculty and staff donated a dollar every Friday for "Dress Down for the Kids Day," and other donations poured in as the event drew closer.

A week before the dance marathon began, an urgent plea came from one of the families. Their twin boys had leukemia, and one needed a bone-marrow transplant. A donor had to be found, but the process for finding a match was painful and costly. Students by the hundreds stood in line and paid twenty-five dollars each to have their blood sampled. No donors were found.

The marathon began at 10:00 A.M. on a cold Saturday morning. Over a hundred dancers filed into the recreation center, now transformed into a playground of games, music and food. Little kids were everywhere, some in wheelchairs, some wheeling IVs around, some with only a tiny layer of fuzzy hair on their heads. Dancers whirled by in T-shirts that said, "I'm dancing for Kristen." Morale volunteers brought candy and gave foot massages as the night wore on.

At the thirty-first hour, the families assembled on stage to tell their stories. Some had children who were too sick to attend, some had lost children only days before. A four-year-old clutched the microphone and stood on tiptoe to say, "Thank you for raising money to save my life."

Then the parents of the twin boys took the stage, alone and holding hands by the microphone. The room fell silent. Exhausted dancers stood up straight. Into the hushed room the parents said, "Tonight we are here alone because our son is getting ready to go into surgery tomorrow morning. Earlier today a bone-marrow donor was found." Then they could no longer speak. With tears streaming down their cheeks, they mouthed the words "Thank you."

Then a group of students assembled on stage holding pieces of posterboard, each with a number painted on it. Slowly they held them up to reveal the total amount that the Dream Team had raised: $45,476.17. The crowd went wild, dancers started running around the floor and families were crying. Everyone knew it had been thirty-two hours of miracles.

Diana Breclaw

Piano Music

There are advantages and disadvantages to coming from a large family. Make that a large family with a single parent, and they double. The disadvantages are never so apparent as when someone wants to go off to college. Parents have cashed in life insurance policies to cover the cost of one year.

My mother knew that she could not send me to school and pay for it. She worked in a retail store and made just enough to pay the bills and take care of the other children at home. If I wanted to go to college, it was up to me to find out how to get there.

I found that I qualified for some grants because of the size of our family, my mom's income and my SAT scores. There was enough to cover school and books, but not enough for room and board. I accepted a job as part of a work-study program. While not glamorous, it was one I could do. I washed dishes in the school cafeteria.

To help myself study, I made flash cards that fit perfectly on the large metal dishwasher. After I loaded the racks, I stood there and flipped cards, learning the makeup of atoms while water and steam broke them down all around me. I learned how to make y equal to z while placing dishes in stacks. My wrinkled fingers flipped many a card, and many times my tired brain drifted off, and a glass would crash to the floor. My grades went up and down. It was the hardest work I had ever done.

Just when I thought the bottom was going to drop out of my college career, an angel appeared. Well, one of those that are on earth, without wings.

"I heard that you need some help," he said.

"What do you mean?" I asked, trying to figure out which area of my life he meant.

"Financially, to stay in school."

"Well, I make it okay. I just have trouble working all these hours and finding time to study."

"Well, I think I have a way to help you."

He went on to explain that his grandparents needed help on the weekends. All that was required of me was cooking meals and helping them get in and out of bed in the morning and evening. The job paid four hundred dollars a month, twice the money I was making washing dishes. Now I would have time to study. I went to meet his grandparents and accepted the job.

My first discovery was his grandmother's great love of music. She spent hours playing her old, off-key piano. One day, she told me I didn't have enough fun in my life and took it upon herself to teach me the art. My campus had several practice rooms with pianos where music majors could practice. I found myself going into those rooms more and more often.

Grandma was impressed with my ability and encouraged me to continue. Weekends in their house became more than just books and cooking; they were filled with the wonderful sounds of the out-of-tune piano and two very out-of-tune singers.

When Christmas break came, Grandma got a chest cold, and I was afraid to leave her. I hadn't been home since

Labor Day, and my family was anxious to see me. I agreed to come home, but for two weeks instead of four, so I could return to Grandma and Grandpa. I said my good-byes, arranged for their temporary care and returned home.

As I was loading my car to go back to school, the phone rang.

"Daneen, don't rush back," he said.

"Why? What's wrong?" I asked, panic rising.

"Grandma died last night, and we have decided to put Grandpa in a retirement home. I'm sorry."

I hung up the phone feeling like my world had ended. I had lost my friend, and that was far worse than knowing I would have to return to dishwashing.

I went back at the end of four weeks, asking to begin the work-study program again. The financial aid advisor looked at me as if I had lost my mind. I explained my position, then he smiled and slid me an envelope. "This is for you," he said.

It was from Grandma. She had known how sick she was. In the envelope was enough money to pay for the rest of my school year and a request that I take piano lessons in her memory.

I don't think "The Old Grey Mare" was ever played with more feeling than it was my second year in college. Now, years later, when I walk by a piano, I smile and think of Grandma. She is tearing up the ivories in heaven, I am sure.

Daneen Kaufman Wedekind

Ten-Dollar Bills and Roses

Once a week, every week without fail, the envelopes arrived. Each college student from the small church received an anonymous envelope. Inside was a hand-written prayer and a brand-new, crisp ten-dollar bill.

When Abigail was moved to a nursing home, friends made a great discovery. They found a shoebox that contained a list of college students from her church, as well as envelopes, some leftover stamps and a few brand-new, crisp ten-dollar bills.

Word got out among the members of the congregation. Soon after, each college student sent one carefully wrapped red rose every week, with a handwritten prayer attached.

Abigail unwrapped each of the packages every week. She told the staff she was as proud of her "prayer charges" as if they were her own children, had she been blessed with them.

She never thought of herself as childless. She and dozens of former college students knew differently. After many years of giving anonymously, Abigail was rewarded with love and appreciation, one rose at a time.

Mary J. Davis

A Not-So-Random Act of Kindness

I have seen many astounding acts of kindness during my twelve years of speaking to over two million college students on more than one thousand college campuses.

Students pitching in to collect money to send a student home to see his mother who was dying of cancer.

A blood drive to aid automobile victims near campus.

Fraternity men who go once a year to the retirement home near their chapter to dance with the older ladies the day before Valentine's Day.

Who could doubt the generosity and goodness of college students! Despite media reports to the contrary, college students care deeply about others and the world in which they live.

But one event, though small in national stature or international importance, touched my heart. At Bethany College in West Virginia, I was speaking at a dinner for student leaders, with my five-year-old son, J. J., sitting next to me. After twelve years on the road, I now take one of my children—Christa, Samantha, J. J., or Hannah—with me on every trip. I have just gotten tired of being away from them.

We were eating dinner, when my son made a strange

reptile-like sound and deposited his dinner on the table at what could have been called, up to that point, a semi-formal event. It is hard in life to always think of the other person when you are dealing with your own agenda and personal embarrassment. In this case, however, I was able to "get over myself" and realize that the little guy was in trouble. We caught the subsequent "blasts" in a bucket quickly provided by one of the students and actually finished the meal—though those with a view of my son's problem passed on dessert!

The big question I then encountered was what to do with his clothes. Being a guy, I reached the conclusion they would be thrown away, justified by the reality that we were traveling and leaving for Cincinnati that night. Suddenly I heard a voice that I now realize belonged to an angel, or perhaps a saint, standing next to me.

She said, "Give me his clothes, and I will wash them during your speech." She was a student at the dinner, she seemed sincere, and I immediately began to question her sanity. Who takes someone else's very dirty clothes and washes them, willingly? We all know it is bad enough doing your own clothes or those of someone you know and love.

"You don't have to do that. I couldn't ask that of you," I said.

"You did not ask," she stated. "And that Tigger sweat-shirt is his favorite," she said.

"How do you know that?"

"Tigger is my favorite, too," she replied, "and he and I talked about it during dinner."

I realized then that I had been wrapped up in myself and missed their entire conversation. I knew, too, that I was dealing with an extraordinary young woman who wanted to reach out to someone in need, even though she had never met us before. As she left with the clothes in a trash bag, I turned to her mentor and said, "She is really something. What year is she?" He said, "A freshman, and what you have seen is a regular occurrence with her."

When something silly happens on a campus now, or even a bad thing takes place, I think of that young woman, armed with J. J.'s clothes in a bag, heading for her residence hall. She gives me hope because I know there are others like her. Students who are good and kind—persons who will be in charge of the world my children will grow up in. That night I was theoretically the teacher . . . but in reality, she was my teacher, and I was her humble student.

That is the beauty of being an educator. If you are open to the possibilities, there is a good chance that we will exchange roles at times and grow together. Dean Robert Schaffer of Indiana University once said, "I have to believe that the student's life will be better because we have met rather than if we had not, because I know how much richer my life has become because of my students."

One fall night in Bethany, West Virginia, my life became richer, my purpose empowered, my spirit lifted because of a not-so-random act of kindness by a wonderful college freshman.

Will Keim

Christy's Last Day

Do not wish to be anything but what you are, and try to be that perfectly.

Saint Francis DeSalas

I did it. Finally. After four years of struggling, studying, and working nights in the library to help pay my tuition, there were only thirty seconds of the last minute of the last exam of the last class of my college career. All I had to do now was traverse the campus to my car and drive home to start my new life—as a college graduate. It was all downhill from here.

Well, maybe not. Halfway across campus, my heel broke. I continued limping and suddenly what was otherwise a sunny day began to cloud over. Was that a drop of rain I just felt on my cheek? What next?

By the time I reached my car, I was drenched. So much for my new life being filled with sunshine. I was forty-five minutes late for margaritas. And there was a lot of traffic. I guess everyone else was in a hurry to get home and start their new lives too.

I negotiated the maze of parking lots and drove to the

edge of campus. One more traffic light to go and *fiesta*. The light turned green but the car in front of me didn't move. The driver began to honk. Then he swerved around whatever was blocking his path and sped off. I began to do the same when I realized that the obstruction was a man in a wheelchair. In fact, I recognized him as one of my fellow classmates whom I had seen many times over the past four years, but never spoken to.

But I was in a hurry. I had important celebrating to do. I began to drive off. I glanced in my rearview mirror and saw the man struggling to get his chair out of the muddy intersection.

Surely someone else will help him, I thought.

But what if everyone else thought that, too?

I stopped.

His name was Jordan. It was difficult to understand this at first. His cerebral palsy affected his speech. We tried to get his wheelchair into my college student's econo-box but to no avail. If I was going to help him, it meant pushing him to wherever he was going, in the rain, in the mud. I like to think of myself as a nice person, but surely there were limits. After all, I did stop when no one else did. I did try to get his chair in my car. At least I got him out of the intersection.

As I was sorting through this moral dilemma, I looked down at Jordan. He was shivering in the rain. But he was smiling. For some reason, he didn't seem to mind. He clearly didn't expect me to do more than I had already done. He began to wheel off down the muddy sidewalk. I couldn't leave him now.

I locked my car and quickly caught up to him. I began to push. It was uphill for what seemed like a mile. Every hundred yards or so, with great effort, Jordan would crane his neck around so that he could look up at me in appreciation. *How could I have even thought of leaving him?* I thought.

At the end of our long trek to Jordan's apartment,

which was the closest disabled person's accessible building to campus, both of us were soaked to the bone and drenched in sweat. I couldn't believe that Jordan had managed to do this alone, every day for four years. To think I threw a minor tantrum every time I couldn't find a parking space close enough to my classes! Jordan insisted that I come in and dry off. He said there was someone he wanted me to meet.

I was a little afraid to go inside. I don't know what I expected. I hadn't ever been to a disabled person's home before. I guess I was afraid of the unknown. When I got inside, I was a little ashamed of my fears. Not only was I surprised, I was impressed. Jordan's apartment didn't look like any ordinary college student's slovenly habitat. Instead, it was a modicum of efficiency and good taste. Each item was carefully placed and within Jordan's reach. And so many books!

"Have you read all these?" I asked him.

"One a week for the last four years," he replied.

That, in addition to his studies! He reached for my hand and motioned for me to follow him to the back bedroom. He knocked gently and whispered something through the door. I followed him inside. He introduced me to his bedridden mother whom I later found out had suffered a stroke some years earlier. Chair-bound Jordan, full-time college student and avid reader was also her primary caretaker.

Jordan left us there and went to make some tea. I wasn't sure if his mother even knew that I was in the room or if she understood what Jordan had just told her about the chair and the rain. But suddenly she raised up her head and began to speak.

"In four years," she said, "not one person has ever helped my son. It's not that he needs help, but it gets lonely out there sometimes."

I didn't know what to say. Margaritas seemed like such a distant thought now.

I stayed for dinner. Jordan and I celebrated our last day of school together. In all those classes and after all that studying, I learned my most valuable lesson off-campus.

Christy Calchera
As told to Dan Clark

The Gift of Music

I had been inside the prison called Gander Hill several times already by the time I met Ray in the spring of 1993. My father worked there with a group teaching inmates to improve their communication and speaking skills. I was a senior in college, majoring in speech communications, and eventually I started my own volunteer student group at Gander Hill.

Teaching communication means getting people to tell their stories, but Ray could tell you how much he missed playing his guitar without speaking. Sometimes he moved his hands across the air as if he were playing his favorite blues scale. He always gave me a slight nod when he saw me come into the chapel for the meeting. He loved sharing his guitar stories. Although he had been an inmate at Gander Hill for over a decade, he always had a song in his head, in particular one that he said he had been writing in his mind since his arrival. He looked forward to playing again the way a child counts the days until summer vacation.

When my group formally established itself at Gander Hill, the men were allowed a night of celebration to which they could invite one or two family members. The night of the celebration was just like Christmas for them. They huddled with their loved ones, whom they had not seen or touched in several months or longer. Since his family lived in Texas, no one came to the celebration as Ray's guest, but he waited patiently for me to arrive. As he rehearsed his song in his head, I walked into the prison with a guitar.

Ray tuned that guitar as if he were putting his life back into harmony. I have never heard a guitar tuned like that before or since. He looked at me over his shoulder and nodded a thank-you before bringing his song to life on the guitar. I watched Ray's fingers dance across the strings as if they were himself, running free. And for those few moments, he was.

Brandon Lagana

Our Community

One Tuesday evening in the beginning of the fall 1996 semester at Shippensburg University, sirens sounded. These sirens were not in celebration; they were a cry to the university that something was wrong. A house, only one block away, was on fire. Nine of the university's students lived there.

From the minute the word got out that help was needed, it seemed like everyone showed up. The victims of the fire were offered endless invitations for housing for the night. The very next day, everyone got into gear to do their part in helping them. Flyers were posted with items that were immediately needed, just to get these students through this next couple of days. Boxes for donations and money jars were placed in every residence hall.

As a residence director, I went before the students in my hall to ask them to do what they could. I knew that college students don't have much, but I asked them to do their best: "Every little bit will help." I really didn't think they could do much. I was proved wrong.

At the hall council meeting the night after the fire, my residents decided to have a wing competition, where each wing of the building would team up to see who could bring in the most donations. I announced that the wing that won would receive a free pizza party.

Thursday evening we announced over the PA system that we were beginning the wing competition. Within minutes, the place exploded. The single large box that I had placed in the lobby was overflowing. We quickly grabbed more boxes, and we watched in amazement as they, too, filled to the brim. Members of the resident assistant staff and I began to count the items. I was astonished by what I saw, and I was inspired by these kids.

When we came to the final tally, the winners turned to me and announced that they would like to donate their winnings as well. They wanted the victims of the fire to have their pizza party.

Tears welled up in my eyes. I had watched these students jump to action, work tirelessly and donate all that they could. And then, as if that were not enough, they handed over their reward. I was touched and so very proud of them.

Christa F. Sandelier

7

FRIENDS

The most important function of education at any level is to develop the personality of the individual and the significance of his life to himself and to others.

Grayson Kirk

The Kids in the Hall

People love others not for who they are, but for how they make us feel.

Irwin Federman

When I started applying to colleges, I definitely had no idea what I wanted to major in, let alone what kind of career I wanted. All I knew was that I wanted nothing to do with math or science. So I researched liberal-arts programs and found myself at Emerson College in Boston, a school known for its music, television and theater departments.

Because I'd been writing fiction since I was fourteen and had appeared in every school play since junior high, I thought I was more than prepared for what Emerson's brochures called a "creative environment." But when I stood outside my dorm that first day in Boston and saw my fellow freshmen in all their vintage, multipierced, tattooed glory, I realized I was wrong. I suddenly felt about as alternative as Mariah Carey. All these intimidatingly artsy guys and girls, lugging crates filled with tons of CDs, paints and sheet music, looked like they had grown up on a different planet from me and my Gap-packers back in suburbia. I was sure I would want to transfer before Thanksgiving.

Back at my preppy high school in New Jersey, you could be labeled weird if you weren't wearing the "right" loafers. So when I started to meet the people who lived on my floor—like the girl with the electric-blue hair who walked around campus with a hand-carved walking stick and the sorceress a few doors down who said she practiced witch-craft and had dated Axl Rose—I didn't know how to react. The strangest part of it was that a "normal" preppy girl like me was the bizarre one among all these eccentrics—like someone wearing a bathing suit at a nude beach.

After a day or two, I realized I was stuck at this freak show of a college, and there was nothing I could do but try to make friends. So I swallowed the lump in my throat and started classes.

Luckily, the ones I started taking, like voice and articulation and creative writing, kept me busy and absorbed. Once in a while, I saw people in the study lounge who looked like they actually bought their clothes in a store instead of at a garage sale, but they were usually hunched over their computers for hours (wearing invisible but obvious *Do Not Disturb* signs). So I closed my door at night and quietly tried to recite monologues, draft plots for short stories and deal with one of my roommates, who was mostly interested in applying gobs of punky makeup to her face, looking in the mirror every second and going out to flirt with guys.

At night, when I briefly left my room to go to the bath-room or use the vending machine, I began to notice that a scruffy little group (especially a guy who wore a wool ski cap twenty-four seven and a girl who was always draped in long, flowy hippie gear) would gather every night in the hallway. They held miniature poetry slams, played guitars and listened to discs I had never heard before. They talked about human injustices in Bosnia and Tibet, while they lolled around for hours on the beaten brown carpet that blanketed the wide hallways of our one-hundred-year-old stone dorm.

I didn't get these people. My high-school friends and I never read poetry together or jammed, let alone talked about politics. When we wanted to have fun, we went to the mall or saw a movie. And when we talked, we talked about guys—or each other. It occurred to me that even if these people invited me to hang out with them, I wouldn't know what to say. "How late is the library open?" seemed really lame.

But after a couple of weeks, I felt a little jealous of these people who weren't hyper about studying and were getting close enough to talk about everything. Through my open door, I heard them going on about silly stuff like their mutual love of roller coasters. Other times they'd be discussing their deepest family problems. Listening to them form their friendships in the dark hallway was like reading a good book: the plots and mysteries were unfolding before me, but I couldn't take part in the action.

I don't know what possessed me, but one day when I returned from class, I started to sing "Blood and Fire" by the Indigo Girls superloud, straight from my gut, with my eyes closed—and my door open. When I opened my eyes midway through the song, the guy with the ski cap was standing in the doorway. I was mortified that he had caught me singing about how life isn't worth living after getting dumped. But then I thought I might look like an even bigger loser if I couldn't finish the song. He stood there, absorbing me for a few minutes. Then, without a word, he walked away.

It wasn't until I headed for the bathroom and heard him

strumming "Blood and Fire" on his guitar that I waited in his doorway and then mustered up the courage to introduce myself.

The guy in the ski cap now had a name—Marc—and he urged me to come and hang out in the hall that night. He played his guitar, and I sang softly, making up melodies and lyrics. I was so intrigued: Marc was unlike any guy I had ever met. The guys at home were either jocks or nerds. Marc was neither. In my eyes, he was a new kind of male species.

That night he also introduced me to Monique, the long-haired, flowy-skirted girl. She played the cello and knew from the time she was, like, eleven that she wanted to be a filmmaker. She told me that when she was sixteen, she chained herself to the steps of her hometown theater to protest the local government's plans to tear it down. I couldn't believe it. Let's face it: while Monique was passionately involved in the cultural issues of her town, my friends and I were obsessed with *Melrose Place*. I felt shallow, but Monique didn't see me that way at all. She told me that she loved to listen to me sing and that my grave voice inspired her to take up electric guitar.

Some of our other dorm mates began to join us in the hall, including Rob, a tall, beautiful African American guy who also had been too shy to hang out at first. Rob told us stories about growing up in New York City, witnessing drug deals and shootings. We both wanted to be writers, and we started writing goofy scripts about the other kids on our floor (our personal favorite: "The Witch Girl's Blind Date"). Rob turned me on to Coltrane, and the jazz saxophonist's unpredictable seductive recordings became my favorite hanging-out music.

For the rest of our freshman year, Marc, Monique, Rob and I sat up late and talked for hours and hours. The best part of our friendship was that we worked hard on keeping it real. If I was pissed off at Monique, we'd talk about it instead of doing that high-school, behind-your-back thing. And if Rob and I didn't agree on an idea or if I didn't want to go to the dining hall with Marc, they'd be cool about it. It didn't take long for me to tell the three of them all about me—from my parents' divorce to my dreams of becoming a famous singer.

But Marc was my favorite new friend, and I have to admit, halfway through fall semester, he had changed from my hall buddy to my crush. He would call me at 3:00 A.M. to try to lure me outside to sit by the Charles River (yes, we did venture out of the dorm). Sometimes he even called in the middle of the night just to read me a poem. Marc could find beauty in anything—like a dance beat in a Madonna ballad that most people would denounce as cheesy or not even hear at all.

Marc was open to everyone's ideas, no matter how wack. He was even respectful of some of the other dorm inhabitants who tried, with their Ouija board, to channel the one-hundred-year-old spirits who supposedly haunted the place. He would say, "Well, it's their dorm, too" and grin. I haven't met anyone as nonjudgmental since.

It didn't take me long to realize that I was learning more from my new friends than from some of my lectures. Understanding and becoming friends with different types of people was the biggest achievement of my freshman year.

Sure, I can tell you about the beginnings of Western civilization and how to write a speech—but the most important lessons I learned in college probably didn't take place during class. Those lessons were reserved for my dorm room.

Suzanne Casamento

My Sanctuary

It is three in the morning on a Tuesday, and I'm walking toward table eighteen, the one I call home. I pass the waiters, give a brief nod to the regulars and take my seat. I order the "usual," water and peanut butter pie. Yes, I'm at an all-night diner.

I start to take out my books, knowing full well that I will be stuck on the same page of Socrates that I've been on for the better part of the semester. Of course, it's early—for my group that is. I wait for the empty chairs around me to be filled.

Just as the Muzak songs start to repeat themselves, Shana and Jenny walk in. I am greeted with the usual big hugs and smiles. Suddenly, the diner stops being a twenty-four-hour restaurant with bad service and becomes my place—my home away from the prisonlike confines of my drab cell, a.k.a. my dorm room. For the next couple of hours, we will joke about people we know, talk about books, muse on the meaning of life, quote movies and create new private jokes. Table number eighteen is our inner sanctum.

During my senior year of college, I started going to the diner for a reprieve from a dorm room that felt like it was closing in on me. Not to mention the phones, the stereo and the computer. How could anyone seriously expect to have good study habits? Some friends of mine told me about the place; they went there to study, and they really liked it.

So I tried it. It felt remarkably freeing. I started going there every night (except weekends, of course), and, believe me it was not because the pies were that great either. Maybe it would force me to pry open my books, and my grades would improve. Right? Well . . .

But that's not the point. I mean, anyone who has gone to college knows that it's not only about forcing yourself to wake up at 7:45 A.M. (after you had gone to sleep two hours earlier) to listen to a professor spoon-feeding you information regarding the significance of the Battle of Hastings. It is also about finding a little haven where you can create what will be the most important thing in your life—yourself. At a school of thirty-five thousand people, I found a small place that was as familiar to me as my Social Security number.

That place was the diner. It was where advice on dating and anything else flowed freely. Where we would get nutty with exhaustion and no one minded. There was a time I spilled water all over myself, and we laughed until we cried. There were the victory laps over acing exams.

Through laughter, tears, learning, growing and the occasional free ice cream, we found a sanctuary. A place where we could be ourselves.

Eric Linder

My Friend Kim

I'd seen her around campus long before I pledged the Kappa Sigma fraternity the winter of my sophomore year. I'd admired her from afar—the epitome of the untouchable college beauty. I'd decided that if I were forced to choose one perfect girl, she would be the one. Even though our paths crossed several times a day, I felt as if she lived in some remote corner of a distant universe. I was sure she had no clue I existed.

She was there the night, several weeks into my pledgeship, when I was invited to join the brothers at a local honky-tonk. A favorite band was playing that night, and I welcomed the chance to get out of my stuffy dorm room and away from the grind of studying.

I arrived late and took a seat at a table alone in the back of the room. The others didn't notice me from their front row of clustered chairs near the stage, but I didn't care. I was in no mood to socialize with the same slave drivers who made me scrub the floors and take out the trash. I made a pact with myself to hang out for fifteen minutes and then beat a hasty retreat.

I heard a familiar laugh. . . . Then I saw her. She was sitting among them, and I wondered who had made her laugh, wishing it had been me. She seemed to shine, making everything and everybody else in the room fade to insignificance. I looked around and wondered if anybody else saw her, but they all seemed too caught up in their corners of conversation to notice. How could they not? She was stunning. Radiant. I discovered that if I shifted my chair a little to the left, I had a clear view of her. I could watch her surreptitiously—the band in front of her providing the perfect cover.

I imagined myself sauntering up to her and asking her to dance. What would she say? Would she just laugh or simply look right through me? Maybe my voice would crack, and I'd turn and slink away as if it had all been a mistake. Then I could simply spend the rest of my college years going around corners and taking roundabout routes to avoid seeing her.

At that moment, she turned toward the back of the room—her eyes searching as if she'd felt my thoughts on her. I blushed bright red when her gaze rested on me. I saw her lean over and whisper something to one of the brothers, and then she got up and weaved her way back through the cluster of tables. She was coming toward me.

For a moment, my heart began to race, thumping so violently I was sure she could see the fabric on my shirt moving. I looked over my shoulder and saw the "Restroom" sign. I breathed a sigh of relief. Who was I kidding? I took one last sip of my ginger ale. It was time to go home.

"Hey, Rob, what are you doing back here all by yourself?"

I looked up, and she was standing right in front of me. She was smiling as if we'd known each other all our lives. I swallowed hard. My voice vanished into thin air. She pulled out a chair and sat down at my table.

"How'd you know my name?" I finally managed to mumble, several octaves higher than normal.

"I asked around," she said with a twinkle in her brown eyes. "I always make a point of knowing the names of all the cute guys on campus."

I flushed a deep crimson, and even though I'm sure she noticed, she didn't mention it. She took a sip of my ginger ale and began to talk. She told me all about herself. Where she grew up. What her family was like. Her favorite movies, what she liked to eat, her hopes and dreams and disappointments. Fifteen minutes turned into a half hour, an hour became two. We talked and laughed like old friends. There were people all around and a band playing somewhere behind us, but I'd long since lost consciousness of the din of voices, the music, the smell of smoke. We'd slipped into our own world—one where a new friendship was being born.

By the time the band finished its third encore, Kim Lattanze had stepped off the pages of my imagination and into my life. She hugged me good-bye at the door and walked off into the night.

We became the best of college friends in the months and years that followed. On graduation day, we hugged good-bye and promised to always stay close. At first, we kept our pledge with cards, letters and numerous phone calls. Sometimes we'd run into each other at some alumni gathering or football game. She'd take me by the hand and pull me to a corner, where we'd take up right where we left off as she'd pepper me with questions about my family, career and love life. We'd always leave with a promise to be a little better at staying in touch.

But soon the times between promises grew longer and longer, and our paths took us in different directions. She moved to Atlanta and became a buyer for a department store, and I eventually packed up and drove to California to try my hand at screenwriting.

Fifteen years later, my thoughts sometimes still drift

back to those college days. I recall an evening—a moment kept alive in the memory of Kim's smiling eyes. One small but unforgettable minute in time. A shy boy, a beautiful girl and the precious gift of friendship she'd brought to my table that night.

And now, when I invariably find myself scanning the corners of rooms at parties, I stay vigilant—always on the lookout for that timid stranger who might feel a little out of place, a little left out. I can recognize myself in those bashful souls, and then I think of Kim. What would she do in a situation like this? I walk over and say hello.

Robert Tate Miller

819 Gaffield Place

A run-down, off-campus student house in a family neighborhood, 819 Gaffield Place was where Zoe, Judy, Lisa and I lived during our senior year at Northwestern University. The shingles were covered with yellow and brown chipped paint, and the roof was the pale, cloudy color of chocolate milk. A worn white sofa sat on the porch among piles of mail and coupons delivered to anyone who had ever lived there, and two bicycles were chained to the stair rail. To our neighbors it must have looked like a perpetual garage sale, but to us it was home—one that was always a soothing sight to me.

One night I walked there from my boyfriend's apartment after a fight. It was 2:00 A.M., silent and dark, but as I turned the corner past Philbrick Park, the lone street lamp illuminated Gaffield in the distance. I started to run, wanting to be there, to feel safe instead of empty. The curly numbers of "819" came into view. When I opened the glass door and saw the first-floor light, tears welled in my eyes. I burst into the living room.

"Uh-oh," said Zoe when she saw my face. Grabbing her car keys, Judy said, "Slurpees." The others put on their sneakers. We always dealt this way with breakups, failed exams and bad news from home. There was something reassuring about a Slurpee always tasting the same no matter what time it was or which 7-Eleven we went to.

After driving to the all-night 7-Eleven, we headed for Lake Shore Drive, our favorite ride. Lake Michigan was calm outside the car window; inside I was comforted within the cocoon of my friends.

I would be okay.

I had not always felt okay. As a child growing up in New York City, I was often lonely. On Sunday mornings, I sat in our sleek, white Formica kitchen hoping my mother would wake up and make waffles with raspberry jam and maple syrup. But my parents, tired from late Saturday nights, stayed in their room with the door shut until noon.

Then, my parents divorced when I was twelve, and my mother moved out. Months passed between her visits and calls. Though I lived in my father and brother's world of football games and boxer shorts, what I really needed was someone to do my nails with, and talk girl-talk and cry to.

At our house, there was no such thing as being late for dinner because most nights I ordered from a pile of take-out menus. A "family dinner" meant we all ordered from the same restaurant, but we still ate separately, each one of us watching television in our own bedrooms. I knew the string of deliverymen who brought our dinners better than any neighbors.

So I was ready for Gaffield. I first saw the cozy house during my junior year when I visited a friend who lived there. Immediately, I arranged to live there next, and Zoe and Lisa were interested. To afford this house, we needed a fourth. The current Gaffield girls suggested Judy, who they knew was eager to move in. But Judy and I didn't like each other. A year before, she had dated a guy named Billy for a few months. Then I dated him. It turned out he cheated on each of us with the other. Billy was out of our lives, but the jealousy and resentment lingered.

"You're a lot alike," said our mutual friends.

"It's a big place. You'll hardly see her," said Zoe.

I wanted the house and warily agreed. We moved in on a June day after the resident seniors graduated. The price for all their furniture and dishes was fifty dollars—exactly what they had paid the girls before them and the price as long as anyone could remember.

For the first few weeks, Judy and I made stilted small talk when the four of us were together and avoided being left alone. One night I was boiling water for tea when Judy came into the kitchen to make popcorn. We proceeded in silence for several minutes. Finally, she spoke. "This is ridiculous. I don't care about Billy anymore."

Startled, I burned my hand on the teapot. "Me neither," I said.

"But," she paused. "There are a few things I want to know." We talked for hours, sitting on the wooden countertop with a bowl of popcorn between us. My other friends had always dismissed Billy as a jerk or a phony, but Judy understood his allure and the pain he could cause. It felt so good to say what I wanted and to stop pretending that things were fine. When Zoe and Lisa came home and found us together, they began talking quickly, trying to break through awkwardness that was no longer there.

"It's okay," Judy interrupted. "We talked about everything."

The four of us had already lived in the same house for almost a month, but that night marked the beginning of our life together. We started developing rituals and routines. We had bagel breakfasts, walked to class together, grocery shopped on Wednesday nights. Returning from class on rainy days, I would count the slickers on the porch railing to see who was home. In the fall and winter,

Sunday dinner was pizza, and in the spring we barbecued on the porch. But the best time was meeting at home at the end of each day.

One night I was late for dinner because I had a meeting with my American-literature professor. On my way home, I imagined Lisa, who loved to cook, at the stove in our kitchen and Judy, who preferred to watch, asking, "Isn't Michele's class over at five?" I walked faster. The second porch step made its familiar sigh as my foot landed on it.

"We were worried," said Judy when I walked in. Everyone was in her seat at the table beside the large window. The fourth chair was empty with a place set. My shoulders relaxed. I was back in my spot.

As seniors with most of our credits complete, we didn't feel guilty about cutting our afternoon classes. We would walk down the alley to buy tomato soup or candy at the deli and rent movies from the video store. We would spend the afternoon in the living room by the brick fireplace or on the plump sofa covered in blue velour worn to the color of a spring sky. We talked about everything, from what we were learning from our majors to what we were learning about sex. I knew whose boyfriend liked red lingerie and whose preferred none. When my boyfriend said, "Don't tell anyone," the Gaffield girls didn't count. I saw them as an extension of myself; nothing I told them would go beyond our circle.

At times like that I felt that we had become a kind of family. I realized family doesn't have to be your relatives—family means that your life is part of someone else's like sections of hair that need each other to form a braid. Often I raced upstairs to my journal to record these scenes. Most of the entries ended with, "This won't last forever."

But in some ways it has. Seven years later, we all live in New York and see each other every few weeks. Recently, two nights before her wedding, I handed Lisa the blue

satin garter I had worn at mine. On it I had sewn a piece
of pink ribbon on which I wrote "The Gaffield Garter" in
indelible ink. As the first of us to marry, I decided to pass
my garter along. I know sisters who have such wedding
traditions, and my old roommates are my sisters.

Occasionally, we talk about visiting Gaffield, but we
haven't. We don't want to see other people's raincoats
hanging on the porch railing or another car parked in the
alley. We don't need to see that creaky house—it is inside
each of us.

One mention of Gaffield, and all our faces relax with a
softness usually reserved for remembering a first love.
Recently, when I was giving blood, I felt faint and had to
look away from the needle. "Think of something pleasant," said the nurse. "Like the Caribbean or ice cream."

Like Gaffield's rainy day smell or the softness of the
blue sofa. Like seeing the curly numbers come into focus
as I hurried down our street and ran up our porch steps.

That's my something pleasant, now and always.

Michele Bender

An Unlikely Hero

Adversity reveals genius, prosperity conceals it.

Horace

When Dr. Gullickson was assigning project mates for his introduction to experimental psychology class, I secretly hoped he would pair me with a cute coed or at least a classmate I could have some fun with. Above all, I hoped he wouldn't assign me to work with the intense, fiercely competitive, singularly serious fellow who always wore dark clothes and apparently had a personality to match. As fate would have it, Dr. Gullickson very deliberately matched everyone in class and announced that I would be working with the one person in class I wanted to avoid.

I went up to my new lab mate and introduced myself. He looked at me as though I weren't there. I felt he treated me as though I would hold him back and probably cause his grade-point average to take a nosedive. He wasn't outright mean or abusive. He just gave me the impression he could do whatever project we dreamed up better if he did it alone. He was a loner, and I could only impede his research. He had important things to do, and I was going to be something of an annoyance he'd have to deal with.

Needless to say, I didn't look forward to an entire semester of being brushed off, but I tried to make the best of it and didn't say anything, lest I make things worse.

The project required each lab team to develop a hypothesis, set up an experiment to test the hypothesis, run the tests, do the statistical analysis and present the findings. Whatever grade the team received would be shared by both students. When my lab mate and I met to discuss our project, I was uneasy. Here was this challenging student who had a reputation for single-mindedness and good grades—the exact opposite of me. I was outmatched. I actually wanted to drop the class at one point, but stopped short because I didn't want to give him the satisfaction of my chickening out. I asked my friends at work what I should do, and the overall response was to stick it out no matter what.

After lengthy discussions, we somehow agreed to do a study on the tactile-kinesthetic perception of space. I wasn't sure what it meant, but at least we had a topic. We started to meet regularly to formulate our plans, and every time I felt the project was more his than mine. The more we met, the more I resented his intelligence and his ability to cut through to the core issues. And I was aware he was much more advanced than I. He knew technical things and approached every detail with great singularity of purpose.

I, on the other hand, must have seemed naive, with little to offer. At one point I summoned up my courage and asked him why he seemed so uptight and serious. To my surprise, he replied that he didn't have time for small talk or petty people and things that would waste his time. He even went on to say that he didn't have many friends because most so-called friends were just a distraction. But, he added, when he did choose someone to be his friend, they would be a friend for life. I was floored by his cold and cynical response. Right then and there, I realized the end of the semester couldn't come soon enough.

As the semester wore on, we tried to fashion a simple yet elegant experiment. Part of our job was to select students who had volunteered to be subjects for our project. I decided to devote myself to the task of working with the subjects, while he developed the scientific model. I put in my two cents' worth whenever I could, but I still felt he was the driving force.

Then one day I got word that he was in the hospital. Apparently, he had been admitted for a hemorrhaging ulcer. The stress of getting the best grades, holding down a job and helping his girlfriend through the medical crisis she was going through had taken its toll on him.

When I visited him in the hospital, I noticed for the first time a sense of vulnerability on the face of my stoic lab mate. I knew that he was aware that I could blow the experiment, and our shared grade would shatter his lofty G.P.A. and possibly derail his chances for graduate school. I assured him I would not let him down and he should only concentrate on getting better. I would do my best. We both knew I'd have to do better than my best.

I had a formidable task ahead of me. I was in over my head, running the statistical data. I poured more time and energy into that project than I had ever done on any assignment in my life. I was not going to let him see me fail and have it reflect on him. I was working the graveyard shift at my job, so I used whatever quiet time from midnight to 6:00 A.M. to work on the project. The work consumed me. There was a sense of challenge that completely overtook me. The question remained: Was I up to it?

Eventually, the semester came to a close, and each team had to present its findings in front of the assembled class. When it was our turn, I did my level best to present his scientific methodology with my showmanship. To my amazement, we were awarded an A!

When I told my lab mate about our shared triumph, he smiled and thanked me for carrying on. Something connected then. Something special. It had to do with trust and the exhilaration of sharing a common prize.

We have stayed close throughout the years. He went on to achieve a doctorate. He also went on to marry his college girlfriend.

I learned more than statistical analysis and experimental procedures that semester. My life has been enhanced by our encounter and challenged by this man, who became my unlikely hero.

And in the end, he was right: we have become friends for life.

Tony Luna

With Help from a Friend

*Cherish your visions and your dreams, as they
are the children of your soul and the blueprints
of your ultimate achievements.*

Napoleon Hill

I remember the first day of classes at Parsons School of
Design. How awkward I felt and how self-conscious! Were
my clothes right? My hair? My talent? Was I good
enough? Was I gonna cut it?

I walked in and scoped out the room while holding my
breath. My vision scanned and then sharply stopped on
one person. Wow. She looked cool. I plopped myself down
in the empty, waiting chair next to her.

"Hi, I'm Dorri." I don't remember what I thought would
actually happen, but I do remember being thrilled when
she smiled a big white toothy smile and said, "Hi, I'm
Kathleen." That was all it took.

What a difference Kathleen made in my college life! She
was confident where I was shaky. She was disciplined while
I was wild. She was responsible; I was lazy. We signed up for

all of the same classes. I was so impressed with her. She worked with incredible diligence and with such self-assurance. I started to emulate her. I wanted to impress her.

One day the homework assignment was to create an exciting illustration based on a pair of shoes. I was bursting with ideas and ran home and pulled out my favorite pair of antique thrift shop "old-lady shoes." I concentrated and worked and sweated and created a self-perceived masterpiece!

I called Kathleen and bragged that I'd finished the assignment. "What?!" she exclaimed. "How could you possibly be finished already?" I was so pleased with myself that I asked her if I could run by her apartment and show her my stunning creation. "Sure," she said.

I raced down from my fifth-floor apartment, precious drawing in hand, and headed to her place. When I got there, I held up my paper with such glowing confidence, only to have my swelled cockiness crushed by Kathleen's reaction: "Is that the only drawing you did?"

"Well, yes," I responded sheepishly. "Why?"

"C'mon," she said. "It's still nice out. Let's go to Washington Square Park and really do some drawings." I was puzzled, but when she led, I willingly followed.

The whole way to the park, Kathleen animatedly talked about form, content, composition and really studying your subjects. She described the shoes in my drawing as the kind you see on the old women that sit in the park and feed pigeons. Her excitement was contagious.

When we got to the park, she surveyed the scene and chirped, "Over there!" She pointed to a bench that was surrounded by discarded, crumpled paper bags, soda cans and empty cigarette packs. An old woman sitting on the bench had fallen asleep. Kathleen handed me her drawing pad and said, "Here. Now, draw the shoes on that woman! Draw them over and over until you really know what they look like."

I drew and drew. I filled the sketchbook pages. They were the best I'd ever done thus far. Kathleen watched, and I felt fueled by my captive audience. I was showing off! It was such fun.

The next day was the class critique. I felt so proud hanging my drawing up on the wall for all to see. I knew I had drawn an illustration to be proud of. As the class discussion circled the room to my piece, I heard my fellow students say, "sensitive," "accurate," "beautifully stylized." I looked over at Kathleen, and she gave me that wink and loving smile of hers. College was going to be a lot more fun with her around.

And it was. She continually inspired me, laughed with me, sketched with me and went out dancing with me. Our works of art were chosen for special exhibits, and we both made the dean's list. We wore our caps and gowns together, and a few years later, I was "best woman" at her wedding.

Whatever fears I had going into college about not being able to make new friends were gently washed away when I found my special, best friend.

After we obtained our B.F.A. degrees, the world opened up for both of us. Now we are both successful self-employed artists. Me, a freelance illustrator and graphic designer. Kathleen, a sculptor and mural painter. I work in my lovely Chelsea cooperative apartment that I bought five years ago. Every morning I wake up grateful for how life has turned out. I make myself a cappuccino and enjoy sipping it as I sit at my computer.

Oops! I gotta run. Kathleen and I are meeting for dinner and a movie.

Dorri Olds

$\overline{8}$

TOUGH STUFF

*Each time something difficult and challenging
has happened to me it has marked the
beginning of a new era in my life.*

Kimberly Kirberger

My Star

My head plopped down right in the middle of my open calculus book.

Maybe the information will just work its way into my brain through osmosis. I was beginning to think that was my only hope for learning this material. I felt like I was on a different planet. *How could this seem so foreign to me?* Of all the classes that I had taken so far in college, I could not make this one work. I couldn't even lay out a logical study plan. *What now?* I pondered, with my head down on my desk in the middle of class.

When I lifted my head off the page, unbeknownst to me, a Post-it Note had stuck to my bangs. There was a pretty picture. I turned to face the guy next to me; he laughed and reached over to pull the note off my bangs in hopes of retrieving some of my dignity.

That was the beginning of a great friendship. The guy who was willing to pull a sticky note off my hair would soon become my calculus savior. I didn't know it at the time, but Matt Starr was the literal "star" of the class. I was convinced he could teach it. And, as luck would have it, he was willing to help me.

He lived in an apartment just off campus, and I would

go over there for tutoring. In exchange for his help, I cleaned his apartment and brought over bribe treats. Cookies, snacks, even dinner sometimes. He was so smart and would get so involved in the material. He would say, "Don't you realize that this is the stuff that the universe is made of?" Not *my* universe. I told him that my universe was made up of child development and psychology classes and an occasional shopping mall, not equations like this. He would just laugh and persevere. He was convinced that he could get me to understand this material, and in a way he was right. He was so crystal clear in his understanding that I began to see it through his eyes.

Matt and I started spending more time together. We would take long walks, go to movies—when he wasn't forcing me to study. I helped him put together a very hip wardrobe, and he taught me how to change the oil in my car—something every girl should know. When I brought home a B in calculus, we celebrated for three days.

Throughout college we stayed as close as a guy and a girl who are friends can be. We dated, only briefly, but the chemistry we shared was more like that of a brother and sister. We did, however, help each other through our other various and odd relationships; and when it looked hopeless, like neither one of us would ever find a mate, we took the next logical step—we got a puppy. Having rescued it from the pound, we called this little shepherd mix Tucker. We had been spending so much time together that when I moved out of my dorm, Tucker, Matt and I became roommates.

The day he came home and told me he was sick, it was raining. It rained that entire week, almost as if the world was mirroring our tears. Matt had AIDS.

Two weeks later, he was in the hospital with pneumocystis. The hows and the whys didn't matter when we were both spending every moment trying to get him better. Between taking final exams, figuring out medications, visiting healers and making Matt drink wheatgrass juice, I was exhausted—but he was getting better.

Matt and I decided that we were going to make the time either one of us had left on this planet count. By the time we arrived at our senior year, I had lived life more fully than I had in all my twenty previous years. When we graduated, we all proudly wore our caps and gowns, Tucker included. Two months later, Matt went home to Minneapolis to live with his family.

Life continued; we e-mailed each other voraciously. I sent him tons of JPEG images of Tucker and his antics, and we went back and forth recounting stories of our lives.

Matt lived only two years more. When I got the news that he had been taken to the hospital, I flew out to be with him. By then, he had fallen into a coma from which he would never awaken. At the funeral, I artfully arranged a yellow Post-it Note in my hair and put one of Tucker's favorite chew toys in the casket.

One night, about a year after Matt's funeral, Tucker and I were driving in the hills of Mulholland. Suddenly, I smelled something so very familiar to me, and yet I couldn't place it. It was a lovely cologne-like fragrance. Then Tucker began acting peculiar.

"What's the matter, boy, did you smell it, too? What is that smell? I just can't place it."

Stopped at a red light, I looked up at the night sky and Tucker barked. What I saw next amazed me. It was a shooting star. A star! Of course, Matt Starr! It was his cologne I smelled.

"Is our friend trying to say hello and tell us he's okay?" Tucker started wagging his tail furiously. Whether it was a sign or not, I felt the warmest and most secure feeling I've felt while thinking about Matt since his death. The giant gaping void that was created when he left was suddenly filled with that warm love the two of us always shared. He wasn't gone, he was right here with me, as he always would be.

Suddenly and quite clearly, I understood how it all fit together. The universe, my friend and his beloved calculus.

Zan Gaudioso

Independence Day

I can still hear our prepubescent voices calling out to one another in the camp's swimming pool. Back in the days when getting our ears pierced and owning Cavarichis determined whether we were cool, the closest we came to cigarettes was fake smoking with pretzels.

We were children who thought we knew everything but really knew very little. Stubborn, we believed the New Kids on the Block and Vanilla Ice were the coolest groups around and couldn't fathom our tastes ever changing, ourselves ever changing.

The years passed. We graduated from high school and went off to different colleges, where we did change. Some of us became vegans, others atheists. We changed our majors, from Spanish to communications to international relations . . . and some of us began toweling our doors so the RAs wouldn't detect we were doing hands-on experiments for our drugs and human behavior class.

I suppose I shouldn't be surprised that my childhood friends have grown up to smoke everything that doesn't smoke them first. I remember my elementary school had a representative from D.A.R.E. (Drug Abuse Resistance Education) come and warn us against the dangers of drug use. He explained about everything from shooting heroin to huffing common household products. Apparently his warnings backfired, for I recollect one of my classmates inhaling a bottle of Wite-Out during recess.

It's not that I expected everything to stay the same. In fact, I welcomed change and was eager to go off to college and begin a new life. I knew some of my friends and I would grow apart, but I never could have predicted how I would feel when I saw one of them snorting coke.

I was visiting a friend at her college and had become aware of changes in her since high school. She now smoked like a chimney, which was actually mild in comparison to the other toxins she routinely put in her body. As she lit up her zillionth cigarette of the day, I made a cancer comment to which she rolled her eyes and flippantly responded, "Well, I guess if I ever get suicidal, I'll be well on my way."

We were in one of her friends' off-campus houses, and, just like the movies, white powder was carefully laid along a mirror and cut with a razor. I was offered a line but shook my head no and watched in shock as my chain-smoking friend expertly snorted one.

Minutes later, bustling with energy, she rambled, "People think cocaine is a really big deal, but now you see it's not. I'm just really happy and alive right now, that's all."

I felt sick to my stomach seeing her like this and high-tailed it out of there, spending the night with a friend who had also declined the drug. Personally, I have found cocaine to be especially terrifying ever since childhood, when I read a *Sweet Valley High* book in which one of Elizabeth Wakefield's friends tries coke at a party and dies of a heart attack. If the writers intended to scare children away from coke while they were still impressionable, they sure accomplished that with me.

I think how we've changed and why we've changed since going off to college, and I've realized some things.

Peer pressure is not like an after-school special where a group of bad kids with a joint surround a younger, smaller kid, saying, "Come on, don't be a chicken. Try it! You know you want to." It's more the internal pressure of feeling like a loser for being scared and wondering whether it can really be that bad if your friends are all doing it.

When you're living on your own for the first time, it's easy to get caught up in the moment. (Just look at the number of college girls flocking to the health center Monday morning for the morning-after pill.) A part of me wants to believe drugs really aren't that big a deal, that you're only young once and yada, yada, yada. But then I see the death tolls of kids my age and sometimes younger. And it scares me—it really does. I see the flashing lights of ambulances, and it seems kind of ironic that drinking oneself into alcohol toxicity is how we try to show our independence.

When it comes down to it, living on your own is about making decisions—not always the right ones, but, hopefully not so many wrong ones that you lose your chance.

Natasha Carrie Cohen

#38 Chucky Mullins

On homecoming day my senior year of college, I was in the stands, surrounded by my fraternity brothers and watching my school, the University of Mississippi, play against Vanderbilt. The game was scoreless late in the first quarter, and Ole Miss had their backs to the goal line. I happened to be sitting parallel to the play action on the field. The Vanderbilt quarterback drew back and passed to the tailback for what looked to be a sure touchdown.

All of a sudden, an Ole Miss defender—football jersey #38, named Chucky Mullins—read the play perfectly and charged the Vanderbilt receiver, hitting him helmet first and jarring the ball from his hands. As I stood up and cheered for the touchdown-saving play, I noticed everyone got up from the ground but #38, who lay where he had fallen.

The Ole Miss trainer ran out onto the field, knelt beside Chucky and asked him what the problem was. "I cannot feel anything, anywhere," replied Chucky.

The emergency medical team immobilized him on a spine board and took him to the small community hospital in Oxford. Once the doctors X-rayed him, they saw the catastrophic damage that had been done to his spine. He was immediately flown to the neurosurgery intensive-care unit at Baptist Memorial Hospital in Memphis, Tennessee, eighty miles away. His status: paralyzed from the neck down and fighting for his life.

The force with which he had hit that Vanderbilt receiver had caused four vertebrae in his spine to fracture explosively. The neurosurgeon who operated on Chucky said it was the worst such injury he had ever seen. The surgery to realign his spine, although successful, left him paralyzed from the neck down without the possibility of a return of function.

Chucky, a sophomore, vowed not only to walk again, but to return to Ole Miss for his degree. Ole Miss officials quickly established a Chucky Mullins Trust Fund and invited contributions from students, alumni and other universities to help meet the phenomenal medical costs, estimated at ten thousand dollars per week.

The following Saturday, Ole Miss was to play Louisiana State University. The student body decided to take up a collection for the Chucky Mullins Trust Fund at that game. So many students signed up that hundreds had to be turned away. The students waded through the stands carrying buckets and trash bags, and collected donations in excess of $175,000.

Chucky, allowed to sit up in bed and listen to the game on the radio, was stunned to hear the announcers describe the outpouring of affection for him. The story was soon being told all over America. Money arrived from every state in the nation. Within a few months, the donations had reached close to a million dollars.

Later that year, the university was preparing to elect its "Colonel Rebel," which is the school's highest accolade. Seven students were in the running. All withdrew their candidacies by writing a joint letter to the dean saying that it was their hope that all students would show their support by voting for Chucky Mullins. Chucky, a poor African American from Alabama, was named Colonel Rebel that year. It is important to keep in mind that this is the same school where federal troops were once needed to protect a single black student who wanted to enroll.

The Ole Miss football team completed the season by defeating arch-rival Mississippi State and gaining an invitation to the Liberty Bowl. Miraculously, only a few months after the devastating injury, Chucky attended the Liberty Bowl game, bound to his wheelchair. Moments before the game, as the players crowded around him, all wearing #38 on the sides of their helmets, he nodded to them and whispered, "It's time." Ole Miss defeated the Air Force Academy that night 42 to 29, becoming Liberty Bowl Champions.

The following year, Chucky sat in the corner of the stands near the players' exit, where each Ole Miss Rebel teammate clasped his hand before taking the field at the start of each home football game. That season, Ole Miss outgained their opposition by an average of forty yards per game, upset one conference powerhouse after another, won a national ranking and gained an invitation to the Gator Bowl in Jacksonville, Florida.

In January, against all odds, Chucky returned to classes at Ole Miss. Although some would call it his greatest achievement, his goal was to eventually get up and walk out of his wheelchair. He would tell reporters, "I know what the doctors say, but I will never quit trying."

Wednesday, May 1, 1991, Chucky was getting ready for class when he suddenly stopped breathing. A blood clot shut down his lungs. He never regained consciousness and died five days later.

All of the Ole Miss football team members were present at the funeral, where he was laid to rest by his mother.

Afterward, some people would say that it might have been better if he had died right away and been spared the suffering. Obviously, they did not understand. Chucky, who came to the University of Mississippi as a poor kid with nothing, changed his world forever.

James Simmons

Zap the Sap!

For me, growth begins immediately after I am able to admit my mistakes and forgive myself.

Kimberly Kirberger

I couldn't believe it. As I walked onto campus I saw posters everywhere with the words "Zap the Sap!" scrawled on them. I was the student body president and I was being recalled from my position. As my peers began arriving on campus, I watched them gather around the posters and then look my way. At that moment, I felt my heart, my character, and my whole body was being pushed back and forth over a cheese-grater. I was in pieces and trying desperately to keep my composure.

When I was elected student body president, campus officials congratulated me on my campaign saying it was one of the best the college had seen. My political career began by throwing Frisbees on the campus lawn. I would throw a Frisbee to someone I didn't know and they would throw it to someone they didn't know. Before long, we had built a community of people who met every day at lunch to throw Frisbees.

One day while throwing Frisbees, the group sponta-
neously decided to climb the mountain near our campus.
When we reached the summit, it felt like we were at summer camp. We laughed, danced and told dirty jokes. It was
intoxicatingly fun. While playing like little children in the
cool mountain air, we unanimously decided to do it again
the following week. Our motto was "Bring a Friend."

So the next week while playing Frisbee, we would
throw it to someone we didn't know, run over and invite
them to climb the mountain with us. We would say,
"Climbing the mountain is better than sex. We guarantee
a climax every time."

We started out with a small group of hikers. But as the
word spread, the number of participants increased. One
day on campus, I met a woman in a wheelchair and we
started talking. Her name was Grace. I asked her if she
had ever been to the top of the mountain. She said she
hadn't. I told her that my buddies and I would carry her if
she were up for it. Grace accepted the offer. The next time
we went up the mountain, we all took turns grabbing a
corner of her chair as we carried her 1.7 miles to the top.

This was probably one of the most magical and deeply
meaningful things I did in college. By the end, we had
over seventy-five people climbing the mountain on
Thursdays, including Grace. All of us who participated
felt like we were part of something much bigger than we
were. We were building a community and it felt great.

With the student body elections approaching, my
friends from the mountain encouraged me to run for
president. So I did. I knew I could make a difference. With
a campaign team of seventy-five people rallying around
me, no one was surprised that I had won the election.

The first thing I did as president was hang a sign outside the Associated Students office that read, "Under New
Management!" I was proud of my accomplishment to say
the least. Most of my life as a youth was spent in the

principal's office for being in trouble and this was one of the few times I had actually achieved bona fide respect and appreciation from my peers.

They say absolute power corrupts absolutely. It sure did in my case. I let all the power go to my head. My ego, my arrogance and my pride were out of control. I began speaking down to people, demanding they listen to me because I thought I knew what was best. My friends and supporters tried to communicate to me that I had changed, that I was abusing my position, but I wasn't listening.

It wasn't long before the very people who had believed in my presidency began to turn against me. But I still wasn't paying attention. I took my obsession with power to such an extreme. A public conflict with the female vice president opened the floodgates for others who were upset with me. It became a blood bath. What started out as a wonderfully enriching experience, or so I thought, suddenly turned into one of my worst nightmares. "Zap the Sap!" posters would soon be everywhere on campus.

When I realized I had made a mistake, it was too late. My whole world collapsed. I had never felt so much pain and sadness in my life as I did then. There I was, one of the most-liked guys on campus, powerful and making a difference, until my ego took over and destroyed everything.

A friend of mine said, "When a man looks into the abyss and nothing is staring back, that is when he finds his true character." I was empty and emotionally bankrupt. I was at the bottom and had nowhere else to go but up. I began to rebuild. I apologized to a couple of die-hard supporters, who for whatever reason did not quit on me, and asked them to forgive me for all the wrongdoing I had committed. They accepted. I told them I was going to fight this recall election. I wasn't just going to roll over and accept defeat.

The campus was in an uproar. Every day the newspaper had an article or letter to the editor saying what a big jerk I was. So I went back out to the campus lawn and began explaining to the students that the allegations were true. I had let the power get to my head and abused my position. I promised that I had learned my lesson and that I was not done serving the students. I wanted to build a coffeehouse on the campus, only the second of its kind in the state. I wanted to build it near the fine arts area and have the theater department do one-act plays, the music department perform concerts and the speech department recite poetry there. I thought to myself, *Please do not recall me. I am not done yet.*

I am not sure if I would have been recalled or not, but, by a stroke of magic or divine intervention, summer came. The charges were dropped and I stayed in office.

The next semester, I had a chance to begin again. As I approached my mission to build the coffeehouse, I was much more humble. I wanted to show the campus and myself that I was worthy of my position. I had never built a coffeehouse before and didn't really know what I was doing, so I asked everyone for help. I asked the students, my advisor, the governing board and the college president.

I used to think that I had to pretend to know what I was doing, that I had everything under control and that I was in charge. It was that kind of thinking that got me into trouble in the first place. Now, I was finding that the easiest way to gain other people's respect was to admit to them what I did not know. I was shocked. It was my not knowing, my humility, and my willingness to ask others for help that was making me win in my new endeavor.

I finished my term as president. In the end, the team that I had put together raised over $125,000 and we built a coffeehouse that is still there eleven years later.

On graduation day, as I grabbed my diploma and walked past my college president, he whispered, "Son, what doesn't kill you makes you stronger."

Eric Saperston

I Said No

I was eighteen years old when I left home for the first significant period of time. As a college freshman, I spent the five-hour drive upstate arguing with my mother about the speed limit and the radio. When we arrived, I was eager for her to depart.

Growing up, I had been shy, reclusive and insecure. I viewed going to college as a chance to wipe that slate clean. Despite my parents' reminder that "we take our hang-ups everywhere we go," I wanted to become an entirely new person, outgoing and confident. I began to introduce myself with my middle name instead of my first, about which I had been teased for years.

I met Brian my first day on campus. A tall, charming senior, this Texan lived right down the hall and helped me move my things in. Although I was suspicious of the end-less string of compliments he drawled, I was also quite flattered. I had never believed I was beautiful, though my family told me so all the time. I didn't date much in high school; just the occasional movie date with this boy or a walk around the mall with that one. I felt special when Brian called out, "Hey, gorgeous" even when I was wear-ing my glasses instead of my contact lenses.

My roommate, Tara, had turned out to be a disaster. Tara was a homesick Bostonian who cried all day about how she should have joined the Peace Corps. Frankly, I also rather enjoyed the idea of her departing for some far-off country. The tension between us made Brian's room a haven of sorts for me. He would fix me screwdrivers, which I sipped while he downed beer after beer and talked about scamming people for money. I knew he was bad news, but at the time that just made him more appealing.

One night he came into my room and lifted me over his shoulder. He carried me, kicking, screaming and laughing, into his room and began tickling me. The next thing I knew, we were kissing.

We began fooling around every day. He was much more experienced than I, who had never done more than kiss. I was upfront about my virginal status, and he said he was fine with it. Then one night things got out of hand.

I remember certain things, like we were watching *The Cutting Edge,* and I was wearing my white ribbed tank top. I had been hinting all week about wanting to discuss "where we stood," but he kept dodging the subject in that sly way of his. It was like pulling teeth, but I finally got an answer—only it wasn't the one I was hoping for. He didn't want a girlfriend because he was graduating in the spring.

I felt stupid and used. All I wanted was someone to love me. We started discussing sex again, but I knew I wasn't ready, especially with someone who wouldn't commit to me. He said there were other things we could do, to which I finally consented, even though I knew it was against my better judgment.

It happened so fast. One minute we were making out, doing "other things," then before I knew it, it was all over. I wasn't a virgin anymore. I was so shocked I couldn't move or speak. I was so angry, so scared, so confused— and I couldn't quite believe it had happened.

After it was over, Brian made me swear not to tell any-one. At that time, I was so humiliated, I couldn't imagine telling another soul. I was sure my friends and family would lose all respect for me because I had sex with a guy I had only known for a short while. It took me a while to accept that what happened to me wasn't sex.

Most of us have a stereotyped image of sexual assault. In the TV movie of the week, rape is about being grabbed in a dark alley by a stranger. It is always violent and always leaves physical scars. That isn't what happened to me. As with most women who are sexually assaulted, I knew my attacker. The scars left by "acquaintance rape" are emotional, yet the scars last just as long as, or longer than, physical scars.

After it happened, I had tests done for STDs and preg-nancy, all of which were fortunately negative. I moved to another dorm, all the way across campus, where I would no longer be greeted with Brian's sheepish, "Hey, kiddo, how's it going?" I talked to my friends. I went to a coun-selor. It's a process, and it makes me angry that I have to live with it for the rest of my life. But it's fading. I am moving past it.

One thing that really helped me was the "Take Back the Night" march on campus, where victims, their friends and anyone opposed to rape joins in a rally. Afterward there was a speak-out, and girl after girl got up to tell her story. It shocked me to see how many young women have expe-rienced some version of what I went through.

All of our stories are different, yet the same. While I wish this had never happened to any of us, it makes me feel better that I can be available to help someone else who may experience something similar.

Natasha Carrie Cohen

The Rest of the Story

Jennifer would have caught my attention even if she hadn't stopped to talk that afternoon. The first couple of weeks in my writing class are always a bit unsettling. The students are a blur of unfamiliar faces, most of them freshmen trying to acclimate themselves to their new environment. When Jennifer approached me with a question after the second day, I was grateful for the chance to connect at least one name with a face.

Her writing wasn't perfect, but her effort was. She worked hard and pushed herself to excel. She was excited to learn, which made me enjoy teaching her. I didn't realize then how much she would also teach me.

One Friday afternoon, a few weeks into the semester, Jennifer stopped by after class. She wasn't clarifying an assignment or asking a question about a paper I'd returned.

"I didn't make it to career day yesterday," she said quietly. "I was at the health center the whole day." I gave her a sideways look, startled. "I'm fine now," she reassured me with confidence. "It was just a virus." Then she was gone.

Two nights later, her father called to tell me that Jennifer would be missing a few classes. She had been hospitalized with meningitis. I heard from him again a few days later, and again after that. Her condition had worsened, he said, and it appeared she might not finish the semester at all.

Jenny remained hospitalized, ninety miles away from home. Her mother stayed by her side, camped out in the corner of a cramped hospital room, sleeping night after night on a chair. In the middle of the night, while Jenny slept, her mother sneaked out—but just to duck down the hall for a quick shower.

Grandparents, ministers and long-standing friends all made their pilgrimages to the hospital room. Jenny's condition grew worse, not better. I was terrified when I saw the pale, emaciated girl who had only ten days earlier radiated life and warmth in my classroom. When her grandparents arrived, she spoke the only words during our visit. "This is my college writing teacher," she announced proudly, in a tiny voice. I remembered what her father had said in his first phone call: "School means everything to Jenny."

A week later, Jenny herself called me to tell me she was on the road to recovery. "I'll be back," she insisted. "I have no doubt," I told her, choking back tears. But around the same time, news reports announced the meningitis-induced death of another student at another school. Jenny sank back into her hospital bed.

Then, five weeks later, I walked into my classroom to find Jenny in her seat, smiling as she talked to the students around her. I caught my breath as her rail-thin body approached my desk, and she handed over all of her missed assignments, completed with thought and excellence. The strength of her will to overcome shone out of her pale, weak, eighteen-year-old face. It would be a few more days, though, before I learned the rest of the story.

Jenny's suitemates, Maren and Kate, were just getting up the Sunday morning that Jenny was dragging herself into the bathroom they shared. She had a horrendous headache and had been throwing up all night. Forty-five minutes later, as the two were leaving for church, she was still there. Maren had a bad feeling about Jenny and asked her Sunday school class to pray for her. When they returned to the dorm three hours later, Jenny was still violently ill. Concerned that she was becoming dehydrated, they decided to take her to the emergency room.

The two girls lifted Jenny up and carried her out to the car, then from the car to the hospital. They spent the next seven hours at their friend's side, tracking down her parents, responding to doctors and trying to comfort a very sick eighteen-year-old through a CAT scan, a spinal tap and myriad other medical tests. They left the hospital when Jenny's parents arrived but were back the next morning when the doctors confirmed that the meningitis was bacterial. By noon, they had the whole two-hundred-member campus Christian group praying for Jenny.

I credit these two young students with the miracle of Jenny's life. That same semester, just an hour away on another college campus, two students found a friend in a similar condition—motionless and deathly ill. Instead of getting him to a hospital, they took a permanent marker and wrote on his forehead the number of shots he had consumed in celebration of his twenty-first birthday. Their friend died of alcohol poisoning. Jenny finished the semester with a 4.0.

I remember being asked as a college freshman who I considered a hero. I didn't have an answer then. Since that time, I've learned that I may have been looking for heroes in the wrong places. Ask me now who I admire, and I'll tell you about a couple of ordinary college students I know.

Jo Wiley Cornell

Stuck with No Way Out

At five feet, three inches tall and well under a hundred pounds I looked at myself in the mirror and thought, *How did I get to be such a pig?* At that moment it struck me, I don't know where the clarity came from, but, looking back on it, I am grateful it did come. I thought, *I need help.* This need for perfection and this compulsive behavior was literally going to kill me.

* * *

When I started college the stress began to take its toll and I started overeating. I was living away from home, I was separated from most of my good friends, and I was in a big school taking premed classes. I was facing many adult responsibilities that came from living away from home for the first time, and my class load was heavy. Food became my comfort, fast food became my excuse—I had to eat! Chips and cookies were my reward for good grades. And, where I had shied away from eating anything closely resembling candy in the past, I now found myself frequenting snack machines and stocking up on candy bars. It was energy food, I told myself. My newfound diet along with my sedentary life of study, all conspired to put the weight on. By the beginning of my sophomore year, I weighed in at 150 pounds. I couldn't believe my eyes when I stepped on the scale at the doctor's office for my yearly check-up. I had gained forty-five pounds in one year.

I was so depressed. I was back home for the holidays. Between the horror in my mother's eyes upon seeing me, the horror in my own eyes when I saw the numbers on the scale, and becoming the butt (obvious pun intended) of all my brothers' jokes, I did what any normal, red blooded, American girl would do: I pigged out for the holidays.

I went back to school armed with every diet book known to man from my well-meaning mother and a handful of recipes (as if I was going to cook). I could handle this. Taking off weight was never a problem for me in the past. What I didn't realize was that in the past I only needed to lose five or ten pounds at the most. I was now looking at trying to take off forty! When it didn't come off as quickly as I thought it would, I became even more desperate. I was hungry all the time, frustrated at my lack of success and facing summer—shorts and bathing suit season?! I don't think so!

My dorm mate convinced me that if I just purged for one meal a day I would see a huge difference. The thought of bulimia terrified me. But she became very convincing in her argument. "Just once a day. You'll get nutrition from your other meals. You just won't be so hungry all the time." She was right in one regard, the dizziness I was experiencing from the lack of food was beginning to take its toll. I needed to pull down really good grades if I was going to get into a good medical school.

Purging one meal, became purging two, sometimes more. The weight was dropping off. I was so excited and encouraged by seeing my waist again, I joined a gym and began to work out three days a week. Between studying until all hours of the morning, running my body ragged on a treadmill and bingeing and purging, I had become a full-blown bulimic. But I couldn't even admit it to myself. I was in denial.

When I went home for a few weeks in the summer, the accolades from my brothers and the sudden, unexpected, visits from their friends, while flattering, only made it worse. I wanted to be even thinner. My mother, however, didn't like what she saw. She was worried about the dark circles under my eyes and the pallor of my skin. Plus, my naturally calm, easy-going personality had given way to a cranky, argumentative nightmare of a person. I exploded when she questioned me about it. "What more do you want from me? I got straight As this term, lost all the weight that you were bugging me about, and I had to do it all living away from home!" My screaming fit gave way to tears and I broke down. The stress had taken its toll. My mother held me like I was three years old again. I felt comforted but trapped. How could I stop this behavior without giving up everything I had worked so hard for? Besides, I didn't want to be fat again—ever.

I assured my mother everything would be all right and I went back to school. I convinced myself that I could handle this problem, but in truth, I couldn't. I would abstain from my purging behavior for only a few days. Because I hadn't changed my eating habits—in fact they were worse—my weight would begin to go up again. I couldn't stand it so I would begin purging again. Even my dorm mate, the friend who gave me the idea in the first place, suggested that I was out of control. Out of control? How could I be out of control when I've never felt so in control of my life and circumstances? I liked everything about this behavior—almost.

Suddenly, I stopped having periods. My body was screaming at me and I wasn't getting the message. I was taking anatomy and biology classes learning everything about the body, except how to take care of my own. One day I passed out in my dorm room while just sitting down studying. That was it. I looked at myself in the mirror and the warped part of me, the part that was responsible for this behavior, saw a girl who needed to lose more weight. But some wisdom forced its way through and I knew I needed help.

I ran over to the counseling office and grabbed the phone number for the eating-disorder hotline. Even though I felt like a grown-up with all these new responsibilities and being away at college, this was my first real adult act.

* * * *

After being in a group for three months, I was changing my behavior. I found my way out of the darkness with people who cared and professionals who were trained. I continued with the group throughout college and received enormous support for all kinds of life-changing situations I faced. I learned so many things from this experience—it's okay to be scared and you don't have to be alone or do it alone. I took all this wonderful information into my practice and it has served my patients and me well.

When I went home for the holidays that year I was glowing. My mother hugged me and I could tell that she was enormously relieved. We stayed up until all hours of the night and talked about everything. By being honest about my circumstances, I had everything to gain. I was back, and, magically—much to my delight—so were all my brothers' friends.

Rosanne Martorella

9

MIND OVER MATTER

The opposite of love is not hate but indifference.

Elie Wiesel

Breaking the Mold

There is nothing in this world that I am prouder of than my ability to feel, to survive and, yes, to be a fool for what I love and believe in.

Jodie Foster

There I stood, in the middle of a campus that more resembled a city than a school. What was I doing there? I felt so out of place, insignificant and small. I had graduated from high school early, left all my peers behind, and now I was facing a whole new world seemingly alone. Besides that, I was painfully shy, and reaching out for help, or even companionship for that matter, seemed a daunting task. I was not the first one to ever go to college, but it sure felt that way. Maybe I just wasn't cut out for it.

It was my first day, of my first semester, of my first year in college, and all I wanted to do was to go back to high school—and so I did. I made an appointment with my old academic counselor. I felt sure that she would have some answers for me. When she suggested I see a career counselor on campus, I thought I would cry. How could that help? She assured me that a counselor would help soothe my transition, as well as be able to help me with my curriculum. I sat there while she called and arranged an appointment for me, then I walked out of her office feeling like the baby bird being given the proverbial boot.

The next day I sat in a hall with a horde of milling students. They seemed so confident and directed and so much older than me. I was hoping that no one noticed me sitting there alone with my lunch sack. Finally, I was called into the counselor's office. She turned out to be a wealth of information, but what about these feelings of insecurity?

"Would you suggest therapy?" I asked.

Her answer surprised me. She suggested that I immediately enroll in a drama class. She noticed my obvious apprehension, but she was adamant about this particular suggestion—so much so, that she marched me over to the drama department and introduced me to the acting teacher. Before I knew it, I was in.

That first week of classes, I pretty much kept to myself. I took part in all those obligatory exercises in drama class that seemed so silly. Be a tree, feel how it feels. . . . I didn't understand how this was going to help, but I persevered. I would still escape from campus when I had a break and go over to my old high school. Even if it was just to sit in the parking lot and eat lunch, it made me feel better. Sometimes I saw some of my old friends. While they were getting ready for all the fun and excitement that their senior year had to offer, I was trying to fit into a strange new world. Maybe I had made a mistake graduating early. I was missing out on all the senior activities. If I had just waited, I wouldn't have had to do it alone; I would have been with some of my friends.

I couldn't figure out how such a disjointed kind of school experience could lend itself to making friends or creating bonds. Each hour, I went to a classroom, miles away from the last one, with different people. Who came up with this system anyway?

Finally, I began to find some solace in my drama class. It was becoming a safe little world in an otherwise austere place. I grew more involved with the scenes we were now doing, and I was assigned a partner, which gave me an excuse to get to know someone. Besides that, I noticed that the teacher gave me roles so opposite of my own personality that they gave me an excuse to come out of my shell. I started looking forward to this one-hour class on Monday, Wednesday and Friday.

The professor believed that the key to playing a character well was knowing yourself. Introspection became the goal over the next couple of weeks. We would lie on the stage in a large circle, with our heads toward the center, eyes closed. There we would explore our childhood, dialogue with our parents, our siblings . . . How did it make you feel? How do you feel now? People were actually crying.

Then we would sit and talk about it. "What happened just then?" the professor would say. "Bookmark that experience for retrieval when one of your characters is crying out for it." Little did I know it, but I was shedding the layers of my own personal shyness by uncovering past experiences.

When Jon Voight came to campus to do *Hamlet,* the entire drama department became involved. Everyone knew that he was bringing actors with him, but he would also be holding some roles open on the off-chance of finding talent at the university. Auditions would be held the following week, open to all. My drama teacher encouraged me to try out. I was terrified, but I thought, if I could just push through this experience, I could do anything . . . maybe even finish college.

The monologues flew; rehearsals were rampant.

Everyone helped everyone else; the excitement was palpable. This felt better than a high-school dance. I was spending less time parked in my high school's parking lot and more time in the drama department. Auditions were held, and while sets were being built, people held their breaths.

The following week, call-back sheets were posted. When I walked into the drama department, there was such a sea of people around the notice, I could barely make my way through. As people started to notice that I was standing there, it was like the way parted for me. I stepped up to the call-back sheet, and there it was as big as day—my name for the character of Ophelia. I was the only girl in the whole school to be called back for that role. Then from behind me, I heard the voice of my drama professor in my ear: "Seems like we have ourselves a star."

And that's what I felt like. My counselor was right. I did need that drama class. The exercises gave me the courage to face myself, and *Hamlet* made me feel like I could do anything. I had become my own star.

Zan Gaudioso

A Better Message

My senior year of high school, I wanted to be a social worker like my older sister, Lynn. She had really inspired me. I wanted to help people, to make a difference in their lives, just like she was doing.

I knew I had work to do because I hadn't really applied myself in high school. It was more social for me than anything else. But I was looking ahead to my future, and I knew that if I really wanted to do this, I was going to need help. I made an appointment to see a guidance counselor, Mr. Shaw.

He listened to my inspired rap as I went on and on about the wonders of a helping career. I could actually help make a difference in the world! Mr. Shaw looked back at me in disbelief. "You're not college material," he said clearly and deliberately. It felt like my heart stopped . . . frozen in the moment of those icy words.

That evening I broke the news to my parents. Seeing how distraught I was, and how sincere I was in really wanting to go to college, they offered to help. They found a small college that would take me if I could manage to get a C average out of the current semester. It was too late. I had goofed around too much, and even my best efforts could not bring up my grade-point average.

My parents were so wonderful and supportive. They found another small college whose financial status would permit anyone to attend. In other words, they would take anyone with a pulse. I felt like such a loser. Mr. Shaw's resounding words came back to me: "You're not college material." And I was beginning to believe it. So much so that I was flunking out—even at this college.

I gave up. I believed Mr. Shaw was right about me. After I left college, I moved home again and starting working part-time jobs. Maybe college wasn't for me. But deep down in my heart I knew that I truly wanted to be a teacher or social worker, and . . . that would require a college degree. No getting around it.

What would I do? I simply had to try again, I had to believe in myself even if no one else did. With all the courage I could muster, I enrolled in a community college nearby and took one course in their night school. I was shocked when I received my grade. I got an A. Maybe it was a mistake or some sort of fluke. I took another course and earned another A. Wow.

I made an appointment to see one of my professors. Things were turning around, and I needed guidance. Dr. Sarah Cohen, my professor in child psychology, told me to relax and enjoy my experience; I was doing very well by all standards. She also said that I was fun, bright and could do anything I put my mind to. Here was an educational expert with a different message. I felt empowered. I was on my way.

I graduated from that community college with honors and went on to earn my B.A. in psychology and my M.A. in psychology from New York University. The very same degree the illustrious Mr. Shaw holds. I felt vindicated.

I realized that choosing who you believe in can change your life. When I believed Mr. Shaw, my life fell apart and there was no way I would ever realize my dream. But when I believed in myself and persevered through seemingly insurmountable odds, I encountered more people who inspired and supported me the way Dr. Cohen had.

As Henry Ford once said, "If you think you can, or if you think you can't . . . you're right."

Carol Grace Anderson

Homeboy Goes to Harvard

As I walked into the building, I heard whispering among them. Hidden behind dark glasses with a red bandanna wrapped around my head, I approached the front of the room. I wore a long, black coat, a blue shirt buttoned to the collar, baggy trousers and black patent leather shoes. I strutted across the stage and bellowed out the words, "How dare you! How dare you look at me as if I am a good-for-nothing low-life doomed to be dead!" I looked around again. Their eyes quickly shifted away as my eyes made contact. It was as if I had a disease.

They were educators who had come to hear a speaker talk about gang prevention and intervention, about the increase of violence in schools. They expected to meet Mr. Richard Santana, a Harvard graduate. Their eyes continued to shift.

"They call me Mr. Chocolate . . . and I'm here to talk to you about life."

I've always known my life was different. My mother died when I was three months old, and my father left before then. I, along with my two older sisters, was moved from foster home to foster home in Fresno, California. My parents were caught in the juvenile-justice system and the welfare system. I am a product of the system. I hated it.

I was introduced to gangs, drugs and violence at an early age. My uncle, a tall, strong man covered with tattoos, came into my life after serving a sentence in the state penitentiary. He was part of the largest institutionalized gang in the state of California. My uncle played an instrumental role in teaching me the rules of the barrio—the school of survival. This, along with drugs and alcohol, gave me strength to deal with the shortcomings of my life.

I grew up fast, and I developed an inner strength that made the homeboys I ran with gravitate toward me, making me the leader of the gang. My homeboys' trust in my leadership gave me courage and a deep sense of comfort. I held them close. I was prepared to die for them.

I was proud of all this, yet I often wondered, *Why can't others outside my gang see the strengths that my homeboys see in me?* Lack of acceptance by adults around me fed my resentment. So I grew intolerant of anyone who denigrated or disrespected me.

Funny thing is that even while I was rooted in the street life—the drugs, the violence, as well as the love and empowerment of being a gangster leader—part of me was elsewhere. I lucidly saw everything my life was about, as though I were looking at my own life and the lives of those around me from a watchtower high upon a hill. This wasn't a single and sudden moment of lucidity; rather I always had this perspective.

From this watchtower, I saw my homeboys' lives growing shorter each day. Whisper, a talented soccer player who was recruited for the U.S. junior team to compete internationally, gave up his dream when he got his girlfriend pregnant. Menso's ability to take pictures of life with his mind and create beautiful artwork through his hands was lost to his love affair with a syringe. I could name more. Despite how affirmed and familiar I felt with the street life, I knew I wanted another way to live.

One day while looking for a job, I dropped by the Chicano Youth Center (CYC), which offered after-school jobs regardless of my affiliation as a gang member. Through CYC, I went to Washington, D.C., for a student-leadership conference and gave a presentation on issues related to gang violence. This marked a turning point in my life—a point when I realized that I could make a positive contribution to society. As a result of this trip to D.C., I was recruited through the Educational Opportunity Program to attend California State University at Fresno.

In college, I learned about my heritage and the sacrifices made by my race. The protest for access to the university and the struggle for equality had a tremendous impact on my perception of life. I grew to appreciate my culture. Yet I was still heavily involved with the violent realities of the streets. I felt split between being a college student and a street thug.

While in my first year in college, I was approached by the campus police and frisked. When I asked why I was being searched, they informed me that they had received a phone call claiming that someone fitting my description had threatened to shoot a professor for not getting an A in the class. When the officers found nothing, I smarted off, "Well, you better get busy 'cause there's this dude looking just like me about to shoot a professor." Naturally, they didn't appreciate my humor.

If they would have checked my student status, they would have found that I was getting straight As. I knew at that moment that I would always be treated differently, dehumanized because of the way I looked. For this reason, I made a commitment to dedicate my work toward breaking down barriers that prevent other homeboys and homegirls just like myself from entering college.

I dress as a gang member, enter a room with an

audience and speak to them on a variety of educational issues; I then take off a layer of clothing to reveal a shirt and tie. I make many people uncomfortable; I have caused many eyes to shift, many bodies to squirm. But by presenting my life story, I have been able to teach others ways in which they can put aside those biases and prejudices that push youth down.

Richard Santana

From the Heart of a Blessed Temple

Black kids from the projects do not go to college
Nineteen hundred and sixty-five,
Was this really the year to come alive?
I asked my guidance counselor, "Can I go?"
Her answer was an emphatic "No!
To college black kids do not go!"
I believed her.
She lied.
She said, "Black kids from the projects do not go to college."
So I didn't.
Thirty years later . . .
She'll never know.
To college I finally did go. (Bachelor of Science, Human
    Resources Management, Master's Degree in Ministerial
    Biblical Studies, Doctor of Divinity Degree in Life
    Concentration: Missions)
Why did she lie?
Why did I believe her?
God had a master plan.
That I truly did not understand.
The next time he or she says to you, "No way, man!"

You tell them for me, and for you . . .
"Yes I can! Yes I can!! Yes I can!!!"

B. T. Thomas

Second Kind of Mind

Thoughts don't have to be "real" or "true" to create failure or success in our lives. They just have to be believed.

My family members were great conversationalists around the dinner table. Certain subjects came up with regularity. One in particular was that some members of my family, yours truly included, were dumb in math. I always heard my name at the end of the family list of the mathematically impaired. After fourteen years of this, I began to accept it as an indisputable and unchangeable fact.

In high school, I failed algebra three times. Eventually, I passed and was accepted to a college in Wisconsin, where I applied for a psychology degree. One small problem stood between me and my degree—statistics. It was a four-hour lab that had to be taken in my junior year. After hearing all the horror stories circulating about statistics, I mentally went into the fetal position. The panic was overwhelming.

One day I was called into my professor's office. Professor Fine, a short, stout man with thinning hair and a perpetual smile, sat on the front of his desk with his feet dangling over the floor. He read my transcript and held up his hands over his head.

"My son, this is your lucky day." I looked up. He repeated, "This is indeed your lucky day. This is where all of your tenacity pays off. You're going to be great in stats." He had a huge smile on his face.

"How's that, Doc?" I asked.

He shrugged. "You have the second kind of mind. Listen. First kind of minds are the kids who do well in algebra but don't get stats. They struggle like crazy in stats. It's a different kind of math that takes a different kind of mind. Second kind of mind is like yours." He held up my grades.

"Didn't have a clue about algebra, but you'll probably get an A in stats. Kids who get algebra don't get stats. Kids who don't get algebra understand statistics with no problem. If you failed algebra once, I'd guess you'd get an A or a B in stats. Think about it, son. You flunked three times. You're gonna be a genius." He raised his hands over his head again. Eureka!

"Really?" I asked, confused.

He jumped to the floor and held my face with his free hand and looked me square in the eyes. "Really, and I'm happy for you. You never gave up, and now it's going to pay off."

I was ecstatic with the news. He tossed my transcript on the floor near the trash can, shook my hand and slapped my back with great enthusiasm.

As I left the old ivy-covered brick building and started across the campus, I looked up to the second-floor window. Professor Fine was smiling, holding up two fingers for "second kind of mind." I smiled back and held up three fingers for "flunked three times." This scene was repeated a thousand times until I reached my junior year. Each and every time, there was a smile of approval on his face, a firm and enthusiastic handshake, perhaps an introduction to another professor during which glowing expectations were repeated.

Eventually, I began to tell my friends how well I expected to do in statistics. This singular change in attitude affected all my grades. With the awareness of my new "second kind of mind," I received the best grades of my life in college. I never believed I would do that well and probably wouldn't have if it had not been for Professor Fine's intercession.

For two years, I looked forward to taking statistics. When the time finally arrived, I did something that I had never done in any other math class—fought for a front-row seat. I asked so many questions I was often called a pest. My statistics book was never very far from me that semester. Also, there was little time for friends and hanging out. I set priorities and stuck to them.

Despite what the professor had said, it was hard work and took concentration and an occasional tutor. It paid off. I received one of only a handful of As that year. Shortly after, I ran into one of the professor's former aides, who said, "Congratulations. Professor Fine tells his really slow students that 'second kind of mind' story." And then he looked at me and said, "You'd be surprised how often it works. The mind is amazing, isn't it?"

JeVon Thompson

Work for Your Supper

My freshman year of college, I worked in the cafeteria. It wasn't my idea; my dad talked me into it. I was attending a small private college, and they had a program that allowed you to eat free if you worked a certain number of hours for the school. My dad caught wind of this and decided it was a wonderful idea. Dad has always been a work-for-your-supper kind of guy.

I balked at the idea. Dad sweetened the deal by telling me that he would send me fifty bucks a month if I agreed to it. Doesn't sound like much now, I know, but then it seemed like a fortune to me.

After the first month, I was ready to renege on the deal. No one had informed me that my duties would include doing enough dishes to fill my dorm room. I didn't know about deep fryers that left you so coated with grease that, no matter how thoroughly you showered later, you were guaranteed at least one really stunning zit. No one told me how bent out of shape the other students got if you forgot they were a vegetarian and gave them a dead animal to eat. They neglected to put a lot of pertinent information in that work-for-your-food flyer.

Without much enthusiasm, I wandered into the school's

kitchen to fulfill my obligation one Thursday afternoon. I looked at the menu for the meal and groaned. Not just french fries, but the much-loved apple cobbler that was baked in trays that weighed about one hundred pounds. I knew I was going home covered in grease and with arms that felt like limp noodles that day.

I was kind of surprised to see the head cook there. Wasn't her shift.

"Why are you here?" I asked over the clanking of the industrial-sized dishwashers.

"Oh, Esther and Rose are both sick, so I'm filling in. I called my daughter, and she's going to come help out, too."

That made me feel a little better. Cook and her daughter were the most genetically joyous people I'd ever met. Working around them made even doing the dishes fun. Almost.

There was a new guy in the cafeteria. I sized him up. Beautiful. This might not be such a bad night after all. He was tall and lean with coffee skin and the deepest brown almond-shaped eyes. I smiled at him.

"Hey, I'm Arlene," I said. "Welcome to the greasepit. You have a name?"

He flashed me a brilliant smile but didn't answer. I looked inquiringly at Cook.

"Exchange student," she told me. "From an African country."

Well, this posed a problem. In a flash of noninspiration, I did a Tarzan impression. "Arlene," I said emphatically while thumping myself on the chest. I then pointed at him. He got it.

"Moshe Suleman," he answered.

I was plotting how I was going to break the language barrier when Cook's daughter arrived. She waltzed in the back door and promptly slipped and broke her arm on the concrete floor. Broke it good, too. There was a bone sticking out. I screamed, Cook screamed. Cook's daughter made noises I didn't know human beings could make.

A very worried Cook pressed the list of things to do in my hand and fled out the door to be with her daughter as she was whisked away in an ambulance.

"You can handle it!" she yelled at me as she closed her car door.

I was not inspired. I walked into the kitchen and looked at my help, the non-English-speaking Moshe, and almost fled in a panic. The natives needed to be fed, however, and I heard small groups of them getting restless in the dining room already.

The first rush of people were ravenous wolves. We were quickly running out of french fries, so I left Moshe to serve while I went to drop more in the fryer. In the five minutes I was gone, Moshe had managed to really annoy one of the special dietary types. She was yelling, and he kept smiling. A smile like that should calm anybody, but it seemed to make her madder. I took over and gave her a no-salt, no-fat, no-meat, no-taste meal for the evening. She didn't thank me.

The second group of people were hungrier than the first. I decided they could help themselves while I made more french fries and had Moshe make some more cobbler. I pointed to the cobbler and pointed to the convection oven while I was lettering a sign that told the hungry people it was self-service. I was in such a rush to get it out in the dining room, I wasn't paying attention to Moshe. When I ran back into the steamy kitchen to dump in more fries, I found that Moshe had thought I had been pointing to the fryer. We were now the proud inventors of deep-fried apple cobbler.

What a mess.

The natives got really restless when I had to explain they would have to wait a half hour for more fries.

The rest of the evening was one big disaster after

another. We ran out of forks, the dishwasher flooded and Moshe put salt instead of sugar into the iced tea. By the time the students slowed to a trickle, I felt and looked like I had been run over by a fleet of dumptrucks.

Finally, it was over. Nothing left but the dishes. Moshe and I did them in companionable silence.

"Hello," said a strangely accented voice behind us. Moshe and I both turned, and I saw a woman standing there who was as beautiful as he was. She broke into a lyrical language, and Moshe answered her. They both laughed.

She turned to me and said, "Moshe would like to apologize for being such a problem. He asks if you would like to have dinner with us."

What could I say? I accepted. With the caveat that Moshe couldn't cook it.

Turned out that klutzy old Moshe was some kind of Ethiopian dignitary's son. A dignitary who apparently had the same ideas about working for your supper as my dad. He took me not just out to dinner, but out to dinner to the best restaurant in the county.

The woman was his sister, and she came along to translate. We all went dancing afterward, and in the morning he delivered me a dozen roses.

Moshe and I didn't become an item; he was already spoken for, but he treated me like a princess all the same. When that boy apologized, he did it with flair. As his English improved, we became the best of friends. We bonded over french fries, you might say.

I'll tell you though, as wonderful as that meal with Moshe was and as much as I loved each delicious minute of it, I felt I had earned it and then some. The next day, I told my dad he was going to have to cough up another twenty-five bucks a month if he expected me to work for my supper next semester.

Arlene Green

I know you're on a tight budget, but it's sort of
annoying when you say "three-and-a-half cents"
each time I eat a french fry.

Catsup Soup

My father learned how to make catsup soup in college. He didn't major in culinary arts; he just learned which waitresses in which restaurants would give him a free cup of hot water and then look the other way while he stirred in their catsup to make his supper.

He was the youngest of nine children from a North Dakota prairie town. When he went to college, he found many people willing to teach him a lesson or two.

Some tried to teach him that he wasn't a first-generation American whose family had given up everything to come to our country in search of freedom. No, he was just another one of those immigrants.

Others decided that his accent didn't mean that he was probably bilingual; it just meant that he was ignorant.

Working five jobs to pay his way through college and sleeping in someone's car when he couldn't afford room and board didn't make him determined; it only made him the poor son of a coal miner.

But my father never learned these lessons. He never learned them because he just didn't hear them.

His inner voice was louder than any words they spoke.

His dreams were so real that to live them was worth the price he paid.

His vision transcended those who would try to keep him down.

My father learned the lessons for his lifetime.

The same lessons he passed on to his students when he had achieved what he set out to do.

To be a teacher.

And teach he did. In the classroom and on the basketball court. His children and then his grandchildren. Executives, CEOs and convention rooms filled with hundreds of people.

He taught what he himself had lived.

That your dreams must come from your heart's deepest desires. Only then will the barriers come down before you.

To know your heart, you must know yourself.

You are who you decide to be, not who other people decide for you to be.

You were created and intended for greatness.

Be noble. Stand on the higher ground.

He taught them to see their possibilities.

And he taught them to see the soup in a hot cup of water and a bottle of catsup.

Cynthia Hamond

Student Super-Saver™

*The highest reward for a person's toil is not
what they get for it, but what they become by it.*

John Rushkin

I still remember my dream car, a 1976 Special Edition Trans Am. It was deep black with gold accents, the same model Burt Reynolds drove in the movie *Smokey and the Bandit.* I'd worked hard during high school to buy it.

Thousands of miles later, while driving down a lonesome country road, I would gladly have traded it for a decent apartment with some basic furniture. Struggling to finish my freshman year at college, I had recently thrown all caution to the wind and proposed to the girl of my dreams. She said yes.

Then reality struck. Flat broke with the wedding just months away, I was beginning to get a taste of that dreaded adult word "responsibility." My goal to finish college seemed to fly out the window. If there was a way to stay in school, marry and still earn a living, I couldn't see it. I took inventory of my few career skills. I could wait tables. I had spent one summer installing sprinkler systems, but winter was coming, so that didn't make much sense. Was there anything else?

A couple of weeks later, driving down the same country road to pick up my fiancée, a brilliant idea sprang from the recesses of my mind. I'd start a publication for local businesses to advertise to my fellow college students, and I'd call it the *Student Super-Saver*. Sure, why not? I once had a journalism teacher tell me that I was one of the best salespeople he'd ever known. I was going to do it. Before you could blink, I was off to the races. And what a race it was.

I contracted with the local newspaper to be my printer and hired a typesetter. That evening I laid out the advertising on my makeshift light table—a large cigar box with a glass-covered hole and a lightbulb underneath. During the day, between classes, I'd head down to Main Street to sell ads to the shop owners there. I was so enthusiastic about my plan that I could barely sleep. I knew Main Street wasn't a good target spot, but I thought it would be a good place to start. I could practice my sales pitch and perfect it before going after the businesses I had earmarked as top priority—those places where I knew the college crowd would hang out.

Even though some of those Main Street shop owners said no with comments like, "I got a son your age. He mows lawns. What's the matter, boy? You too good to mow lawns?" I persevered, and it paid off. I spent extra money to have an artsy graphic design made in full color for the front and back covers. My life was on the line. And I felt that I was ready.

The big day for distribution on campus came, and I rented space in the student union for fall registration. My fiancée and I were met by a tidal wave of students. The more copies of the publication we unbundled, the more we gave away. The minutes turned into hours, and before we knew it, the day was over. We were exhausted, yet thrilled by our sense of accomplishment.

When we left the student union for the first time that evening, we were horrified by what we saw. *Student Super-Saver* papers were strewn from one end of the campus to the other, and none too gracefully. The wind had scattered them over lawns, bushes and sidewalks. Of the 5,000 copies we distributed that day, it seemed like 4,999 had been tossed. We spent the rest of that evening cleaning up the campus and licking our wounds.

With each paper I threw into the Dumpster, my vision of the good life as an entrepreneur vanished. My brief career as a business owner was over. A few months later, the little pot of profit that I did make ran out. Needless to say, my advertisers were not eager to renew. I had to quit school.

Some months passed, and I got married. We managed to rent a little place and even buy some used furniture. But there was no money to finish college, and I needed to work to support my family. My brief publishing career landed me a day job as an advertising rep at a new local radio station, and at night I waited tables.

But I wanted more. I knew that if I tried again, I could make my idea work. I wanted to be a success and finish college and get my degree. The sobering words of one of my college professors haunted my thoughts daily: "The true education of college is to teach you to finish what you start."

My wife and I scrimped and saved and by the summer of 1984, we had enough money to cover the start-up costs for another issue of the *Student Super-Saver*. I was determined to learn from my mistakes. This time I went after businesses who offered something to the students *and* I hit the favorites first. I approached every pizza place, hamburger joint and brew pub in town, the places most often frequented by starving college students. I didn't step a foot onto Main Street. The cover said it all: "Over $589 of valuable coupons and discounts valid all semester long."

The *Student Super-Saver Volume II* was an overwhelming success. My company grew and allowed me to maintain my status as a full-time student. In 1988, my senior year, the Association of Collegiate Entrepreneurs awarded me the "Outstanding Student Entrepreneur of the Year." I had graduated college, and I had fulfilled my dream of making my paper a success.

Fifteen years later the *Student Super-Saver* continues to dominate its market and has never had a semester that didn't surpass the last in revenues and profits. It has truly been the cornerstone upon which my business empire has been built.

Since then I've started dozens of companies, most successful, a few not. I've traveled the world teaching people how to be entrepreneurial. Teaching them what I learned: Believe in yourself, follow your dreams and don't ever give up.

Kevin Van Gundy

If we could get that stuff into a lamp,
we'd really have something.

Dare to Take Risks!

The world of tomorrow belongs to the person who has the vision today.

Robert Schuller

We all have a very special purpose in life, regardless of who we are or where we come from. I truly believe each of us has a special calling in life even though it took me over thirty years to find mine!

Looking back, I realize my parents unwittingly shaped me to be the person I am today. For example, adopting my mother's streak of independence gave me the room I needed to take daring risks later in life. After ten years of working for a major Wall Street bank and slamming into a brick wall, I vehemently said "Enough!" I knew in my heart I could produce results far more outstanding than a clock-punching, nine-to-five position would ever allow.

One day I was scanning through the papers in search of new and challenging Wall Street opportunities. My eyes were immediately drawn to a Merrill Lynch advertisement. They were looking to hire more stockbrokers, and the qualifications listed were clearly those that I possessed. With great excitement, I made some phone calls and arranged to meet with one of the New York City branch vice presidents. Unfortunately, on the day of my appointment, I was ghastly sick with a cold and 101-degree fever that threatened to topple me physically. Yet I knew a golden opportunity when I saw one and was determined to meet with the vice president. We ended up talking nonstop for three and a half hours!

Based on our conversation and the length of the interview, I was surprised and disappointed when, instead of making me an offer on the spot, he instructed me to meet with twelve of his top stockbrokers for further interviews. *Well, maybe that is a good sign,* I thought.

Over the next five months, I met with these twelve people, each of whom invariably tried to discourage me by saying, "You are better off in a safe nine-to-five bank job," "You won't make it," "Eighty percent of newcomers fail within their first year" and "You have no investment experience." Deep down, I felt like a scared dog with its tail between its legs, but I didn't let it show.

The final interview was scheduled on a cold, blustery winter day in January of the following year. Five minutes into the interview, it was obvious the vice president did not know what to do with me. Apparently, it did not matter that I had written a well-researched twenty-five-page marketing plan that exceeded his expectations. It did not matter that his top salespeople were impressed with me, despite the discouraging things they had said to me privately.

In a moment of daring risk and courage that forever changed my future, I looked at him straight in the eye and seized the moment. "Sir, if you don't hire me, you'll never know how well I can do for this firm."

When I realized what I had just said to him, a chill went

up my spine and I thought, *My God what have I done?* The next thing he said was like music to me: "Okay, you've got the job!" But before I could shake his hand and rush home to spread the good news, he added: "... on one condition." My heart sank. "You must first resign from the bank effective two weeks from today, enroll in our three-month training program and then take a stockbroker exam which must be passed on the *first* try. If you fail even by one point, you're out!"

Inside, I shook like a leaf. I gulped at the prospect of taking a huge leap of faith into the unknown. My mouth suddenly went dry. There was never a time in my life when I so desperately needed a glass of water! I remember thinking that I stood to lose everything if I failed that exam, which I had heard was as difficult as the examination for attorneys. I swallowed hard and croaked, "I'll take it." My future was instantly changed from that moment forward!

After passing the exam and receiving my stockbroker's license, I struggled for several months, living solely on commission and eating pasta, peanut butter sandwiches and cereal. Night after night, I burned the midnight oil in search of new clients. I often left the office weary and fatigued, ready to give up, yet somehow returning the next morning to start a new day. It was a grueling beginning during which I had no social life.

One of the most difficult and challenging aspects of being a stockbroker was making the largely dreaded "cold calls." We were required to make phone calls to literally hundreds of prospects each day, many of whom had never heard of us, in an effort to solicit new business. Rejection was a way of life, and I learned not to take it personally. It was all a numbers game. The more people I called, the more accounts I opened. In addition to cold calling, I also had to coddle very nervous clients during roller-coaster stock-market conditions. This was no easy feat!

Eventually, all the hard work paid off. In less than four years, I became one of the top salespeople at my branch and increased personal sales by 1,700 percent. Through continued faith and persistence, I built and managed multimillion-dollar investment portfolios for U.S. clients, many of whom were distinguished men and women from America's corporate boardrooms, wealthy socialites, doctors and lawyers, as well as nonprofit foundations. This resulted in a cover story for *Careers and the disAbled Magazine*, as well as worldwide press coverage on CNN and in numerous newspapers, including the *New York Times*. All this success earned me a six-figure income, a spot in the prestigious Merrill Lynch Executive Club three years in a row and numerous sales awards.

Toward the end of my fourth year at Merrill Lynch, it hit me like a ton of bricks that something was missing. I became spiritually bankrupt and depressed. I thought long and hard about my goals and where to go next.

At one point, I pleaded with God and asked to be led in the right direction. The Source reminded me of the time when I spoke to hundreds of people, while in college as a student leader, and years later, when I won a "Humorous Speech" championship. It dawned on me that every time I had a speaking engagement, I always came out of the experience with a wonderful, energetic, peaceful and magical feeling that was unmatched by anything else I ever did. I instinctively knew God had blessed me with extraordinary public-speaking skills that could enable me to make a lasting difference and transform other people's lives.

After considering my options, I took another daring risk, gave up *everything* and left the lucrative investment business for a more satisfying career as a motivational speaker. A lot of people, including my parents, thought I was crazy. "It is a pie-in-the-sky dream, because it isn't realistic," they said. I paid no attention to those words, and to this day I have never looked back.

The beginning of my speaking journey was eerily similar to what I had first experienced at Merrill Lynch. Once again, I went back to dining on pasta, peanut butter sandwiches and cereal. Working temporary jobs in between long stretches of speaking engagements was both a harrowing and a humbling experience. There were times when I had only a few dollars in my pocket and ate once a day. If everyone did this, it would put the diet industry out of business! To save money, instead of taking the subway to different parts of the city, I walked or rode my bike. Cab drivers were losing money because of me. Meanwhile, to keep my dream burning brightly, I worked hard on creating a personal message that would reflect my collective learning experiences in the world of finance and inspire people to be the best they could be.

Nothing in the world comes close to the satisfying feeling I get when thousands of people tell me how much I have made a difference in their lives by motivating them to take risks, to make necessary changes and to accept themselves as spiritual beings having a human experience!

The core of my message is, "If I can do it, you can, too!" What could be more satisfying than that? And I say that because I have been deaf since birth!

Stephen Hopson

Emma's Ducks

The winter of 1966 hit our university in upstate New York with a ferocity unrivaled in decades. For three days straight, the snow swirled and billowed, burying the isolated campus. Here and there stray groups of students struggled single file against the weather, like ducklings following their mother across a road. The female students in dormitory B were confronted with the same problem plaguing the general population of the university.

"How are we going to get to the cafeteria?" asked one.

"We're not," answered another. "Everything out there is white. You can't see anything."

A gleam came into the eye of the third girl. She shushed the others' whining, saying triumphantly, "Emma could do it."

The whining turned to murmurs of excitement. "Emma!" "She even manages through the city." "We could follow her." "You're a genius!"

The girls whooped, yelled and clapped for joy. They bundled up and excitedly trooped down the hall to Emma's room. They found her in the hallway and cornered her before she could even open her door.

"What's all the excitement?" she asked, smiling.

"Can we follow you to the cafeteria? We're blind in this storm."

They all laughed.

"I suppose so. I'll go first, and you could hold on to each other's shoulders."

"Can we go now?" one girl begged. "I'm starving."

Emma smiled again. "Sure, let me just get Missy ready."

She went into her room and returned moments later with a dog on a harness. The girls lined up obediently at the front door, ready to face the cold. They each placed their hands on the shoulders of the girl in front of them.

Emma opened the door to lead them out. "I guess," she smiled, "you could call this the blind leading the seeing."

And with that, Emma and her seeing-eye dog, Missy, led her troop of hungry ducks to the cafeteria.

Paul Karrer

Consider This

[EDITORS' NOTE: *The following are excerpts from a commencement address given by Bill Clinton at Princeton University on June 4, 1996.*]

Just consider this, there's more computer power in a Ford Taurus every one of you can buy and drive to the supermarket than there was in *Apollo II* when Neil Armstrong took it to the moon. Nobody who wasn't a high-energy physicist had even heard of the World Wide Web when I became President. And now even my cat, Socks, has his own page. By the time a child born today is old enough to read, over 100 million people will be on the Internet.

Just consider the last hundred years. At the turn of the century the progressives made it the law of the land for every child to be in school. Before then there was no such requirement. After World War II, we said ten years are not enough, public schools should extend to twelve years. And then the G.I. Bill and college loans threw open the doors of college to the sons and daughters of farmers and factory workers, and they have powered our economy ever since.

America knows that higher education is the key to the

growth we need to lift our country, and today that is more true than ever. Over half the new jobs created in the last three years have been managerial and professional jobs. The new jobs require a higher level of skills.

Fifteen years ago the typical worker with a college degree made 38 percent more than a worker with a high-school diploma. Today that figure is 73 percent more. Two years of college means a 20 percent increase in annual earnings. People who finish two years of college earn a quarter of a million dollars more than their high-school counterparts over a lifetime.

The older I get and the more I become aware that I have more yesterdays than tomorrows, the more I think that in our final hours, which all of us have to face, very rarely will we say, "Gosh, I wish I had spent more time at the office," or, "If only I had made just a little more money." But we will think about the dreams we lived out, the wonders we knew, when we were most fully alive.

Bill Clinton

All in the Family

I met Eileen, my brother's wife, when I was seven years old. Only she wasn't his wife then. She was an amazing nineteen-year-old with blond streaks in her hair! I loved her immediately. She was exotic and funny and terrified of my parents when she came over for dinner the first time.

This was back in the days of formal meals with lots of forks lined up. Eileen dropped two peas in her lap, then two more and then another one. She thought nobody saw. I watched her wrap them up in her napkin discreetly. After dinner I told her, "I saw the peas." I said I wouldn't tell, though. Thirty-one years have passed, and this is the first time I've said anything to anybody. It's okay—she said I could.

We were talking on the phone the other day, right around her fiftieth birthday. She was trying to describe what fifty felt like. She said that of the women in our family, she didn't feel like the mature one. Brain-wise, she said, my sisters and I had passed her a long time ago. There were times she felt left out.

For my sisters and me, it was the natural order of things: high school, college, grad school. But Eileen worked while my brother went through medical school.

Then she had babies. She chose to be a full-time mother at a time when many women chose careers first. You never saw a person who loved babies so much. You never saw a happier mom.

"And you never knew how I ached," Eileen said.

No, I didn't.

She told me about a ring—the college ring she had gotten right before she had dropped out. She wore it for years but decided one day to take it off.

"A woman at the library recognized it and said she had gone to the same school," Eileen explained. "And so she asked when I graduated. And I said, 'Well actually I didn't.' And she said, 'Well then why are you wearing that ring?' And I thought: This woman is right. I am a phony. I am pretending to be someone I am not."

I never knew this college thing was such a huge deal to her. She used to tease my sisters about "getting to the other side." By the time I got there, she was joking about being abandoned. I laughed right along with her, never realizing.

Now I do. I've been out of school long enough to chase other dreams. I understand what it is to have an unfulfilled promise to yourself. It can seem so tiny to everyone else as to be imperceptible. But so can a grain of sand in your eye.

In lieu of the college ring, Eileen took to wearing her daughter's high-school ring. "I was so proud of Alyson for graduating high school," she said.

Alyson is now in college, studying art. Her younger brother John finished college in two and a half years. Joe, the third child, is a star student in high school. Tom, the youngest, is in the eighth grade. Eileen has always paid special attention to Tom's schooling. For a while there, it seemed as if Eileen and Tom were always doing homework together.

Now she tells me: "I thought I was going to have a nervous breakdown. I was everybody else but me. I lived through my husband. I lived through my kids. I wanted to have control of everybody. I wanted them to live my dream.

"And so I was hell-bent that my kids were going to go to college. They were never going to feel inadequate, the way I did. And that was so wrong. I had to get my own life."

So a year ago, she signed up for two English courses at the college she had left eighteen years before. The first day of class, she put the ring back on. She got books, test dates, assignments. She thought, *There is no way I can do this.*

Well, she got an A and a B-plus in those courses. She signed up for four courses over the summer. Then the following semester, just last September, she signed up for five courses and committed herself to write her senior thesis on Charles Dickens.

She aced all five classes. She aced her thesis. She is about to graduate, at fifty, this spring. She told me she hasn't been this happy since she was nineteen, and she said the happiness is only incidentally about the college degree.

She told me about Joe and John cooking dinner for the family while she was off at class. She told me about Alyson cleaning the house so her mom could study. She told me about my brother tutoring her in chemistry. She told me who volunteered to read her thesis: Tom.

It was because of her family, not despite it, that she was able to make it. And this circle of give-and-take had made fifty the greatest age to be.

Jeanne Marie Laskas

Never Too Old to Live Your Dream

The first day of school our professor introduced himself to our chemistry class and challenged us to get to know someone we didn't already know. I stood up to look around when a gentle hand touched my shoulder. I turned around to find a wrinkled, little old lady beaming up at me with a smile that lit up her entire being.

She said, "Hi, handsome. My name is Rose. I'm eighty-seven years old. Can I give you a hug?"

I laughed and enthusiastically responded, "Of course you may!" and she gave me a giant squeeze.

"Why are you in college at such a young, innocent age?" I asked.

She jokingly replied, "I'm here to meet a rich husband, get married, have a couple children, and then retire and travel."

"No seriously," I asked. I was curious what may have motivated her to be taking on this challenge at her age.

"I always dreamed of having a college education and now I'm getting one!" she told me.

After class we walked to the student union building and shared a chocolate milkshake. We became instant friends. Every day for the next three months we would

leave class together and talk nonstop. I was always mes-
merized listening to this "time machine" as she shared her
wisdom and experience with me.

Over the course of the school year, Rose became a campus icon and easily made friends wherever she went. She
loved to dress up and she reveled in the attention bestowed
upon her from the other students. She was living it up.

At the end of the semester we invited Rose to speak at
our football banquet and I'll never forget what she taught
us. She was introduced and stepped up to the podium. As
she began to deliver her prepared speech, she dropped
her three-by-five cards on the floor. Frustrated and a bit
embarrassed she leaned into the microphone and simply
said, "I'm sorry I'm so jittery. I gave up beer for Lent and
this whiskey is killing me! I'll never get my speech back in
order so let me just tell you what I know." As we laughed,
she cleared her throat and began:

"We do not stop playing because we are old; we grow
old because we stop playing. There are only four secrets
to staying young, being happy and achieving success.

"You have to laugh and find humor each and every day.

"You've got to have a dream. When you lose your
dreams, you die. We have so many people walking around
who are dead and they don't even know it!

"There is a giant difference between growing older and
growing up. If you are nineteen years old and lie in bed
for one full year and don't do one productive thing, you
will turn twenty years old. If I am eight-seven years old
and stay in bed for a year and never do anything I will
turn eighty-eight. Anybody can grow older. That doesn't
take any talent or ability. The idea is to grow up by always
finding the opportunity in change.

"Have no regrets. The elderly usually don't have regrets
for what we did, but rather for things we did not do. The
only people who fear death are those with regrets."

She concluded her speech by courageously singing "The Rose." She challenged each of us to study the lyrics and live them out in our daily lives.

At year's end, Rose finished the college degree she had begun all those years ago. One week after graduation Rose died peacefully in her sleep. Over two thousand college students attended her funeral in tribute to the wonderful woman who taught by example that it's never too late to be all you can possibly be.

Dan Clark

10

GRADUATION

You hold all of our futures in your hands.
So you better make it good.

Jodie Foster

Life Lessons

Members of the Class of 1997, as I stand before you to deliver your commencement address, I am reminded of a humorous story. Unfortunately, I can't tell it, because it's dirty. It's the one about the two guys who are golfing, and one gets bitten by a snake. Ha ha! That's a good one!

But seriously, you are about to leave this high school or university and enter into a new era—an era that, if current trends continue, will be: the future. Speaking of the future, I am reminded of a quotation by Steve Miller, who wrote: "Some people call me Maurice, because I speak of the pompatus of love."

No, sorry, wrong Steve Miller quotation. I meant this one: "Time keeps on slippin', slippin', slippin', into the future." How true, true, true, young people! But by the same token, you must not forget another very important part of your lives: the past. As students, you have spent the past in school, memorizing facts such as who was the ninth president of the United States, and what percentage of the atmosphere is nitrogen. Many times you have said to yourself: "What good will these facts do me in the real world?"

Young people, you'll find that the things you learned in school will be vitally important to your success, provided that you are a contestant on *Jeopardy*. Otherwise they're useless. In the real world, there are few occasions when your boss rushes up to you and says: "Tell me what percentage of the atmosphere is nitrogen RIGHT NOW or we'll lose the Winkersnood contract!" In the real world, it's much more helpful to know things like what the area code for Fort Lauderdale is.

The answer, I am outraged to report, is "954." What kind of area code is that? You are too young to remember this, but there was a time when there were only about five area codes in the entire world, and they all had either a "1" or a "0" in the middle, the way the Good Lord intended area codes to be, as in "212," an area code that came over on the Mayflower. But today, in this "anything-goes" era of drugs and crime and inter-league baseball, ANY random three-digit number can be an area code, and the phone companies, which are all run by Candice Bergen, are adding mutant new ones at the rate of hundreds per day. Do you want to know why the phone companies are so eager to get your long-distance business? Because pretty soon EVERY CALL YOU MAKE WILL BE TO A DIFFERENT AREA CODE, INCLUDING CALLS TO OTHER ROOMS IN YOUR OWN HOUSE, that's why.

Who is going to fight this injustice? Not my generation. My generation is currently occupied full time with applying skin moisturizers. No, it is up to you to take on the telephone companies, and also the companies that make the cardboard food packages that have the little dotted-line semi-circles that say "PRESS TO OPEN."

Let me ask you a question: Have you EVER been able to open a package by pressing that little semi-circle? I didn't think so. Those semi-circles are reinforced at the package factory with titanium; they can easily deflect bullets. NASA pastes those semi-circles on the nose of the Space Shuttle to protect it during re-entry.

Let me ask you another question: Have you ever tried
to wrap leftover food in clear plastic wrap? Have you ever
tried to tear off a piece of that wrap using the so-called
"cutting edge"? If so, did you get a nice, square piece, like
the one the cheerful homemaker always gets in the com-
mercial? Don't make me laugh until saliva dribbles onto
my commencement robe. What you got was a golf-ball-
sized wad that looks like a dead jellyfish. THE "CUTTING
EDGE" CUTS NOTHING, YOUNG PEOPLE! Fact: For
every leftover food item that American consumers are
able to successfully wrap, they waste more than thirty-
seven square miles of plastic—enough to cover all of
Manhattan Island, or the late Orson Welles.

And what is the Scientific Community doing about these
problems, young people? THEY'RE CLONING SHEEP.
Great! Just what we need! Sheep that look MORE ALIKE
than they already do! Thanks a lot, Scientific Community!

Oh, I could go on, members of the Class of 1997, but I
see that the man with the tranquilizer-dart gun is here. So
let me just close here with some inspirational words from
the ninth president of the United States, Steve Miller, who
said, and I quote: "Jungle love, it's drivin' me mad, it's
makin' me crazy."

I blame all this nitrogen.

Dave Barry

"THANK YOU, SIR. I AIN'T NEVER GONNA FORGET TODAY!"

Reprinted by permission of Harley Schwadron.

A Homecoming of a Different Sort

Jeff and I had many conversations during the year, but I will always remember the time he told me about his family. His mother, a loving, caring woman, was the one who held the family together. She died shortly before Jeff graduated from high school. His father, a successful physician, cold and stern in Jeff's words, had firm beliefs that a person would never make a valuable contribution to the world unless they attended and graduated from college by the age of twenty-three. His father had even paved the way for Jeff to attend the same college from which he graduated, and had offered to pay Jeff's entire tuition and living expenses. As an active Alumni Association member, he was excited that his son would someday follow in his footsteps.

Jeff was twenty-seven and a successful business planner at a Fortune 500 company—without a degree. His passion was skiing. When he graduated from high school he decided to decline his father's offer and instead move to Colorado to work with a ski patrol. With pain in his eyes Jeff told me that he still remembered the day he told his father he was going to forego college and take a job at a ski resort. He remembered every word of the short conversation. He told his father of his passion for skiing and for the mountains and then of his plans. His father looked off into the distance, his face became red, and his eyes squinted and bore into Jeff. Then came the words that still echoed in Jeff's mind: "You lazy kid. No son of mine is going to work on a ski patrol and not attend college. I should have known you'd never amount to anything. Don't come back in this house until you have enough self-respect to use the brains God gave you and go to school!" The two had not spoken since that conversation.

Jeff was not even sure that his father knew he was back in the area near where he grew up and he certainly did not want his father to know he was attending college. He was doing this for himself, he said over and over, not for his father.

Janice, Jeff's sister, had always remained supportive of Jeff's decisions. She stayed in contact with their father, but Jeff had made her promise that she would not share any information about his life with him.

Jeff's graduation ceremony that year was on a hot, sunny day in June. As I walked around talking to people before the ceremony, I noticed a man with a confused expression on his face.

"Excuse me," he said as he politely approached me. "What is happening here today?"

"It's graduation day," I replied, smiling.

"Well that's odd," he said. "My daughter asked me to meet her at this address." His eyes sparkled and he smiled. "Maybe she completed her associate's degree and wanted to surprise me!"

I helped him find a seat and as he left me he said, "Thank you for helping me. By the way, my name's Dr. Holstrom."

I froze for a second. Jeff Holstrom. Dr. Holstrom. Could

this be the same person I had heard about over the last year? The cold, stern man who demanded his son attend college or never enter his home again?

Soon the familiar strains of "Pomp and Circumstance" could be heard. I turned around in my chair to get a glimpse of Dr. Holstrom. He seemed to be looking for his daughter amongst the graduates on stage. Speeches were given, the graduates were congratulated, and the dean began to read the names of the graduates.

Jeff was the last person to cross the stage. I heard his name being announced: "Jeff Holstrom, magna cum laude." He crossed the stage, received his diploma from the college president, and, just as he started down the stairs from the stage, he turned toward the audience looking for his sister.

A lone figure stood up in the back of the audience—Dr. Holstrom. I'm not sure how Jeff even saw him in the crowd, but I could tell that their eyes met. Dr. Holstrom opened his arms, as if to embrace the air around him. He bowed his head, almost as if to apologize. For a moment it seemed as if time stood still, and as if they were the only two in the auditorium. Jeff came down the stairs with tears in his eyes.

"My father is here," he whispered to me. I smiled.

"What are you going to do?" I asked him.

"Well," he said. "I think I'm going home."

Vicki Niebrugge

Two Stories for Life

This is a letter from a college student to her mother and father:

Dear Mom and Dad,

I'm sorry I haven't written in a long time, but something I smoked seemed to have affected my eyesight for a while. The problem is better now. When I was in the emergency room I met a really fine man. He gave me some crystals to meditate on, and, well, to make a long story short, you'll soon have your wish of becoming grandparents. Don't worry. He's mature; he's twenty years older than I am and he has a steady job at the hospital. Who knows, we might even get married. I knew that you would want to be the first to know.

P.S. I really didn't do any drugs, and I wasn't in the hospital, and I'm not pregnant. I don't even have a boyfriend. But I did flunk chemistry. I just wanted you to view this problem in proper perspective.

That is an old story that is brought up to date. It is a metaphor for this occasion—a rite of passage, a ritual that you have not experienced before but which human beings have been doing for a long, long time.

I suspect that you know just about everything that you can hold for the moment in the way of information and advice, and you have some time to process that now. So I will not, unlike some speakers, give you advice and tell you about the future. What I would like to give you as a gift is two stories. Stories that you might take with you as a peg to hang on the wall of your life, so that long days after this, when you assimilate the experiences that you had at this institution, you might have this peg to hang it on.

The first story comes from a friend of mine who is a kindergarten teacher—one of the best. She was asked at a teacher's convention if she would have her class act out some myth, fairy tale or other good story. So being the good teacher that she was, instead of deciding herself, she went to the students, her kindergarten class, and said, "The teachers would like us to act something out. What would you like to do?" And after a lot of discussion, not to anybody's real surprise, they picked something very old. A story that the whole human race knows. They picked that classic old chestnut of "Cinderella."

It is interesting to note in passing that no matter when the survey is taken, that remains the most popular fairy tale for all ages. In the United States of America at least.

It was a good choice on the part of the children because there are lots of roles in "Cinderella." And lots of flexibility. So there was this sorting out that had to be done: who wanted to be Cinderella—all the girls wanted to be the princess—and who wanted to be the coachman, and on and on. As the children received a role and sorted this out among themselves, they were labeled as useful in what their role was and sent over to the side of the room. Until there was only one child left: a small kid, tubby, not particularly involved with the other kids in the class—in fact, sometimes teased—sort of a different kid. The teacher could not say why, but he was not quite like the rest. So she said to him—his name was Norman—"Norman, what are you going to be?" "Well," said Norman, "I think I will be the pig." The teacher said, "Norman, there is no pig in the story of 'Cinderella.'" And Norman said, "Well, there is now."

So they left it to Norman as to what was the pig's part. I mean, no one quite knew how to fit a pig into the story of "Cinderella." It turns out that Norman knew exactly what his part was. It was one of the great walk-on parts of all time.

His notion was to go with Cinderella wherever she went and do whatever she did. So Norman was always there—sort of a porcine Greek chorus to the events. Norman had nothing to say, but Norman's face reflected the action of the drama. When things were serious, he was serious. When things looked worrisome, he looked worried. When things were in doubt, he looked anxious. He began to fill the stage with his presence of response by simply sitting there. And at the end of the performance when the princess was carried off to live happily ever after, Norman stood on his hind legs and barked.

In rehearsal this had been troublesome because the teacher said, "Look, Norman, even if there is a pig in the story, pigs do not bark." And Norman said, "Well, this one does."

You can imagine what happened the night of the performance. There was a standing ovation at the end for the pig. Norman, the barking pig, who was, as it turns out, the Cinderella in the story after all.

Word gets around, and people called up the teacher and said, "We hear you have this dynamite Cinderella thing. What is so special about it?" She said, "Well, there is a pig in it—actually a barking pig." And the person on the other end of the telephone would say, "But there is no barking pig in 'Cinderella.'" And the teacher would say with great conviction, "Well, there is now."

I went out to visit Sophia Smith's grave this morning, to see her house, and I realized that she was a barking pig. She said that there should be a college for women, and people said there is no such thing as a college for women. Her response was, "Well, there is now."

I have always thought that the "Cinderella" story was poison—especially the one that is loose in our culture— because it describes a young woman whose position in life is to wait—to wait for the prince, to wait for the fairy god-mother. The sweatshirt that Cinderella wore says, "Maybe something will happen." Norman, the barking pig, is the kind of "Cinderella" story I like, because Norman got up and demanded that there be room for him and his image of himself in this world. And the real fairy godmother was the teacher who recognized the truth that Norman was reaching for and had affirmed his place in the scheme of things. That is a fairy story you can count on.

Hold that thought for a minute—of Norman the bark-ing pig—and let me tell you another story to lay alongside it to take with you.

This past spring I was in a town not much bigger than this one, maybe an hour's train ride south and west of Paris. It is a town I am sure some of you have visited, and I hope in the future more of you will go. This is where the great Gothic cathedral of Chartres is built. It is probably the most magnificent statement in stone and stained glass that exists on the face of this earth.

The story about Chartres again is an old story that needs to be brought up to date. The story goes that some time during its building, in the early days, a visitor from Rome stopped by to see this amazing thing that was hap-pening in this small town. He got there at the end of the day, and he went into the unfinished structure, and he began to bump into workmen as they were leaving. One of them was brushing some stuff off his front, and the visitor asked him, "What do you do?" And the man said, "Oh, I make glass windows." The visitor went a little further and he bumped into someone else who was brushing sawdust off himself. He asked, "What do you do?" The man said, "I am a woodworker. I am making some beams over here." A little further back, someone else was brushing dust off of himself as he headed home for the evening. Again, the question was, "What do you do?" The answer was, "I am cutting some stone."

Finally the visitor got as far back in this great structure as he could go, and there was an older woman with some young people. They were cleaning up and sweeping and putting tools away. The visitor asked this woman who was doing this work, "What do you do?" She looked at these young people, and she looked at the structure rising above her, and then she said, "Me? I am building a cathedral for the glory of God."

She had a perspective on her place in the scheme of things. And though it was not grand by title—not architect, not mason, not stained-glass–window maker—she had a perception of her place in the scheme of things. "Me? I am building a cathedral for the glory of God." She, too, was a barking pig, like Norman—one of his distant cousins.

I give you these two stories to cast a perspective on what you do when you go from this place. This institution at its very finest is in the business of helping barking pigs find their place. This institution in its every part—staff, faculty, parents, students and visitors—is not just a school but part of that human endeavor of building, if not a cathedral for the glory of God, at least an invisible cathedral for the best in the human spirit.

The thing that strikes me about a cathedral at Chartres is, that town was no bigger than this one—thirty-five thousand people, give or take. And they built this incredible thing. The other amazing thing about the building of Chartres is that they started something that they knew they would never see finished. But if they did not start it, it would not ever be finished, and so they began.

I said I would not give you advice, and I would simply pass on that reflection to you. I leave the rest of the thinking that comes from those two stories up to you.

I would like to make a personal request. For my own strange reasons, I did not go on to have an academic degree laid on me. But I am a practical man, and so I would like to request from this class and the administration of this college that you give me the gift of this chair, this very chair, so that long days from now I can sit in it, and it will bring to mind this lovely day, this amazing institution, this sweet life and the remarkable and unforgettable company of all of you.

Robert Fulghum

Humor Them!

One of the requirements of every commencement speaker is that they offer some advice. Well, get ready, here it comes.

Soon you will be leaving the company of those who think they have all the answers—your professors, instructors and counselors—and going out into what we like to call the real world. In time you will meet up with other people who think they have all the answers. These people are called bosses. My advice is: humor them.

A little later you will meet additional people who think they have all the answers. These are called spouses. My advice is: humor them, too.

And if all goes well, in a few years you will meet still another group of people who think they have all the answers. These are called children. Humor them.

Life will go on, your children will grow up, go to school, and someday they could be taking part in a commencement ceremony just like this one. And who knows, the speaker responsible for handing out good advice might be you. Halfway through your speech, the graduate sitting next to your daughter will lean over and ask, "Who is that woman up there who thinks she has all the answers?"

Well, thanks to the sound advice you are hearing today and that I hope you will all pass on, she will be able to say, "That is my mother. Humor her."

Katherine D. Ortega

GRADUATION DAY AT THE
COLLEGE OF HARD KNOCKS.

Reprinted by permission of Dave Carpenter.

Know Where You're Going!

How important is it to know what you want and where you're going? A study of the graduates of one Harvard class thirty years later says it all: 80 percent had no specific goals, 15 percent had ones they only thought about and 5 percent had written goals (dreams with deadlines). The 5 percent, measured by net assets, had not only surpassed the goals they wrote down for themselves but, as a group, had more net worth than the other 95 percent combined. Impressive!

Speaker's Sourcebook II

And over here's Tom. We hired him *right* out of college.

Reprinted by permission of David M. Cooney.

Who Is Jack Canfield?

Jack Canfield is a bestselling author and one of America's leading experts in the development of human potential. He is both a dynamic and entertaining speaker and a highly sought-after trainer with a wonderful ability to inform and inspire audiences to open their hearts, love more openly, and boldly pursue their dreams.

Jack spent his teenage years growing up in Martins Ferry, Ohio, and Wheeling, West Virginia, with his sister Kimberly (Kirberger) and his two brothers, Rick and Taylor. Jack won a scholarship to attend Harvard University, where he majored in Chinese history. Jack played intramural football and was a member of the Harvard rugby team. He was also a member of the SAE fraternity, where he was the social chairman and later the vice president of the chapter.

After graduating from Harvard, Jack pursued a masters degree and a doctorate in education at the University of Chicago and the University of Massachusetts. He taught undergraduate and graduate classes at U Mass, Hampshire College and the School for International Training. He later developed a graduate-education program for Beacon College in Massachusetts.

In recent years, Jack has focused most of his efforts on the empowerment of adult learners in both educational and corporate settings.

For further information about Jack's books, tapes and trainings or to schedule him for a presentation, please contact:

The Canfield Training Group
P.O. Box 30880 • Santa Barbara, CA 93130
phone: 805-563-2935 • fax: 805-563-2945
e-mail: *theresa@canfieldgroup.com*
Web site: *www.chickensoup.com*

Who Is Mark Victor Hansen?

Mark Victor Hansen wants to "Change the World, One Story at a Time" through the *Chicken Soup for the Soul* series.

As a professional speaker he wants to talk to people who care about things that matter and make a difference in listeners' lives now and forever. He has spoken live to over 2 million people in forty countries at over 2,500 speaking engagements.

As a businessman/entrepreneur he wants to save lives, fortunes and futures. He's actively involved in many business interests—dedicated to feeding the hungry, housing the homeless and reforesting our planet with 18 billion trees.

In 1962, Mark created a rock and roll group called "The Messengers" and "played" his way through high school earning $17 per hour—six nights a week.

Mark attended Southern Illinois University (SIU) and was a research assistant to the "Leonardo da Vinci of our time" Dr. R. Buckminster Fuller. Dr. Fuller finished Einstein's "Unified Field Theory", called *Synergetic Mathematics*. Dr. Fuller patented two thousand inventions, including Geodesic Domes, wrote forty books and created World Games. World Games is a simulated model to "Make the World Work for 100 percent of Humanity." Mark loved working with Dr. Fuller and his fellow research assistants on World Games.

While at SIU, Mark was a student leader and student ambassador to India, Thailand, Vietnam and Japan. Mark wanted to stay in school forever—except that when Kent State University blew up, rebellious students did the same at SIU and the school was temporarily closed.

Mark has honorary doctorates from Life Chiropractic College, Cleveland College, Southern Illinois University and Golden State University (closed before it finished its accreditation process).

Mark has coauthored twenty-six *Chicken Soup for the Soul* books, *Dare to Win*, and *The Aladdin Factor*. Additionally, Mark Victor Hansen has authored *Future Diary, Miracle of Tithing, How to Achieve Total Prosperity*, and is busy at work on several new titles.

An autobiographical video called *The Real Me* has been created and highlights Mark's lifetime of achievements.

Mark's audio programs include *Sell Yourself Rich; Visualizing Is Realizing; How to Build Your Speaking and Writing Empire* and *Living Your Dreams*.

Mark has worked tirelessly to help the *Chicken Soup for the Soul* series be the first series to sell one billion copies.

For further information about Mark contact:

Mark Victor Hansen & Associates
P.O. Box 7665
Newport Beach, CA 92658
phone: (949) 759-9304 or (800) 433-2314
fax: (949) 722-6912

Who Is Kimberly Kirberger?

Kimberly Kirberger is the president and founder of Inspiration and Motivation for Teens, Inc. (I.A.M. for Teens, Inc.) a corporation formed exclusively to work for teens. It is her goal to see teens represented in a more positive light and it is her strong belief that teens deserve better and more positive treatment.

She spends her time reading the thousands of letters and stories sent to her by teen readers and traveling around the country speaking to high school students and parents of teens. She has appeared as a teen expert on many television and radio shows, including *Geraldo*, MSNBC, and the *Terry Bradshaw Show*.

Kimberly says that the *College Soul* book has been an amazing journey. In getting close to and hearing from so many teenagers she kept hearing about this very emotionally packed time that begins with application to college and extends through the four-year experience. It became clear to her that this was a time of life that was filled with many challenges and that college students could really benefit from a book like this. For her, it was simply a continuation of a commitment that she has made to teenagers to do what she can to inspire and motivate them while letting them know there are people who believe in them.

Kimberly is the coauthor of the bestseller, *Chicken Soup for the Teenage Soul* and the #1 *New York Times* bestseller, *Chicken Soup for the Teenage Soul II*, as well as *Chicken Soup for the Teenage Soul Journal*. She is also the coauthor of the forthcoming *Chicken Soup for the Parent's Soul* and *Chicken Soup for the Teenage Soul III* and the author of *Teen Love: On Relationships, a Book for Teenagers*.

Kimberly started the Teen Letter Project with Jack Canfield, Mark Victor Hansen and Health Communications, Inc. The Project is responsible for answering the heartfelt letters received from teenagers and also reaching out to teens in trouble and encouraging them to seek professional help.

To book Kimberly for a speaking engagement or for further information on any of her projects, please contact:

I.A.M. for Teens, Inc.
P.O. Box 936 • Pacific Palisades, CA 90272
phone: 310-573-3655 • fax: 310-573-3657
e-mail for stories: *stories@teenagechickensoup.com*
e-mail for letters: *letters@teenagechickensoup.com*
Web site: *www.teenagechickensoup.com*

Who Is Dan Clark?

Dan Clark is a successful businessman, bestselling author, internationally recognized speaker, entertainer and consultant. Achievers Canada and Achievers Europe named Dan one of the top ten speakers in the world! Dan's story and million-dollar business has been featured on over three hundred TV and radio shows, and in *Esteem* and *Entrepreneur* magazines.

Dan is the author of ten highly acclaimed books including his extraordinary corporate management book *Simon Says: Managing From the Inside Out, Getting High: How to Really Do It* (especially for teenagers) and *Puppies for Sale and Other Inspirational Tales.*

Dan is also an actor, songwriter/recording artist and an award-winning athlete who fought his way back from a paralyzing injury that cut short his football career.

In 1982, Dan was named an Outstanding Young Man of America. He was then sponsored by Zig Ziglar into the National Speakers Association where he soon received their most prestigious award designation CSP, Certified Speaking Professional. Since then, Dan has spoken to over 2.5 million people in all fifty of the United States, throughout Canada, South Africa, and in fifteen other countries in Europe and Asia, including the former Soviet Union.

Dan addresses over 150 groups each year. His clients include hundreds of corporations such as AT&T, IBM, Marriott Hotels, Principal Financial Group, Meeting Professionals International, Texas Hospital Association and other professional associations, hundreds of colleges and universities, NCAA & professional athletic teams, school districts and chamber of commerce-sponsored community events.

To receive a full product catalog of all Dan's books, tapes, music CDs, posters, shirts, etc., and/or to receive a press kit/speaker's brochure and demonstration video about Dan's keynote speeches, consulting services, and half- or full-day training seminars please contact:

Clark Success Systems
P.O. Box 58689
Salt Lake City, Utah 84108
phone: 801-485-5755
fax: 801-485-5789
Web site: *www.clarksuccesssystems.com*

Who Is James Malinchak?

James Malinchak is recognized worldwide as one of the top speakers on the college circuit and is a past winner of College Speaker of the Year by *Campus Activities* magazine and the Association for the Promotion of Campus Activities (APCA). He has talked at over 700 colleges and conferences worldwide. James was also named a Consummate Speaker of the Year by *Sharing Ideas* professional speakers' magazine and speaks for youth groups, school districts, college, universities, corporations, business gatherings and associations worldwide.

He is the author of twelve books including the collegiate top-seller, *From College to the Real World*, *How to Be a Great Student Leader*, and is co-author of the audio program *How to Ace College and Land a Great Career*. He has appeared in *USA Today*, *The Wall Street Journal* and numerous other newspapers.

James grew up in Monessen, Pennsylvania, a small steel-mill town near Pittsburgh, where he led his high school to its first-ever state basketball championship. Prior to pursuing a full-time speaking and writing career, James was an award-winning stockbroker whose clients included many famous entertainers, authors and professional athletes. James is also is a contributing author to *Chicken Soup for the Teenage Soul*, *Chicken Soup for the Kid's Soul* and *Chicken Soup for the Prisoner's Soul*.

James mixes enthusiasm and humor with motivational stories to deliver a high content message that will have you "laughing, learning and inspired!"

To schedule James for a speaking engagement for any group, or to order any of James' books and CD programs, please contact:

James Malinchak International, Inc.
P.O. Box 530061
Henderson, NV 89012
(888) 793-1196
To e-mail visit: *www.Malinchak.com*

For Your FREE Special Report: *"7 Simple Action Steps You Can Use Right Now to Achieve More Than Ever Before!"* Visit: *www.YouCanAchieveMore.com*

Contributing Editor

Tony D'Angelo is recognized as one of the nation's undisputed authorities of Personal Leadership for today's young adults aged eighteen to twenty-eight. CNN has hailed Tony as "the personal development guru of his generation" and *SPIN* magazine has compared him with peak-performance superstar Anthony Robbins. Today, Tony serves as the executive director of EmPower X!, Inc. and has spoken to over half a million college students from over five hundred universities and twenty-three different countries. He is also the author of *The College Blue Book* and of the upcoming book, *Most People Die When They're 23, but They're Not Buried Until They're 70: A Guide to Creating a Fulfilling Life in Your Twenties.*

Contributors

Carol Grace Anderson, M.A., is a national speaker and the author of the highly acclaimed new book: *Get Fired Up Without Burning Out!* Carol Grace went from growing up in a tiny eighteen-foot trailer surrounded by circus perform-ers, to become a super motivator. This former psychology teacher had a role in a Paramount movie with Sandra Bullock, toured with Roy Clark, and has appeared on the *Tonight Show.* Through the big life challenges that she has won, she knows firsthand how to get fired up. Carol Grace shares her inspir-ing secrets and unforgettable stories with organizations across the country. Call Anderson Programs at: 888-32-GREAT.

Michele Bender is a freelance writer in New York City. She has written for many publications, including the *New York Times, Glamour, Cosmopolitan, House Beautiful, Family Circle, Ladies' Home Journal, Fitness* and *Jump.* This story is dedi-cated to her dearest friends: the Gaffield Girls. She can be reached at *MBender878@aol.com*

Diana Breclaw is the director of student activities at Hope College in Holland, Michigan. Her professional career has also included working in student activi-ties and residence life at Elmhurst College. But she holds a special place in her heart for her alma mater, Texas Christian University. She earned her master's degree in college student personnel at Bowling Green State University in Ohio where she started the Children's Miracle Network Dance Marathon to help sick children.

Alexander Calandra is a professor emeritus of physical science at Washington University in St. Louis, where he taught from 1948 until 1979. Dr. Calandra received his bachelor's degree in chemistry in 1935 from Brooklyn College in New York. During his tenure at Washington University, Dr. Calandra became known as a critic of the new math reforms, which were popular in the 1960s. In 1969, he also joined the faculty of Webster College as chairman of the sci-ence department where he worked to develop programs until 1980. In 1979, the American Association of Physics Teachers awarded him the highest honor in physics teaching, the Robert A. Milliken Award. He also was honored by the National Science Foundation for the programs he developed for non-science majors.

Dave Carpenter has been a full-time cartoonist since 1981. His work has appeared in such publications as *USA Weekend, Barron's,* the *Wall Street Journal, Forbes, Better Homes & Gardens, Good Housekeeping, First, Woman's World,* the *Saturday Evening Post,* as well as numerous other publications. Dave can be reached at P.O. Box 520, Emmetsburg, IA 50536 or by calling 712-852-3725.

Natasha Carrie Cohen is majoring in psychology and English at Syracuse University, where she is currently writing a memoir and trying to catch life before it goes flying by and she misses her chance to be incredible. She can be reached at *nccohen@mailbox.syr.edu* To see more of her writing, check out her Alice in Wonderland Web page designed by Rich White at *http://web.syr.edu/~ncohen*

David Coleman is known nationwide as "The Dating Doctor." He received the 1997 National Lecture Entertainer of the Year from the National Association for Campus Activities and the 1996 and 1997 Reader's Choice Lecture Program of the Year from *Campus Activities* magazine. He was nominated for six straight years and is currently the number-one ranked entertainer in America by *Campus Activities* magazine. David received his bachelor's degree from Bowling Green State University, Ohio. He is the author of a self-syndicated column on relationships and a book entitled *101 Great Dates*. He is currently working on two more books: *Prescriptions from the Dating Doctor: Answers to the Most Common Relationship Questions* and *When the Heart Is Unavailable: Putting a Stop to Revolving Door Relationships* (with Richard Doyle). David can be reached at *www.dating-doctor.com* or by calling 513-583-8000. He is represented in the college market by Umbrella Productions, Inc. at 407-649-6448.

David M. Cooney's cartoons are published in a variety of magazines including *Mutual Funds*, the *Lutheran* and *Presbyterians Today*. Through the scientific journals that feature his work, his cartoons are seen in over fifty countries. David's cartoons are also published in the *New Breed*, a cartoon feature distributed by King Feature Syndicate. His cartoons run in numerous newspapers under the title *Twisted View*. David lives with his wife and two children in the small Pennsylvania town of Mifflinburg. He can be reached at *dcooney@sunlink.net*

Jo Wiley Cornell is the mother of two young-adult college students and has been married for twenty-five years to her husband, Peter. She is a full-time faculty member in the Haworth College of Business at Western Michigan University, where she teaches informational writing. Jo also owns and operates The Write Choice, a writing/consultation business for grant proposals, business plans, employment and resume counseling, and the development and layout of mental health workshop/training materials. She has self-published two poetry chapbooks *Shadows of My Mind* and *Shadows of My Mind, Revisited*. She is currently working on and looking for a publisher for her nonfiction book, *Tentacles of Depression: Understanding a Child's Pain*, a work that illustrates the devastation of clinical depression as seen through the eyes of a child. Jo can be contacted via snail mail at 3907 Wedgwood Dr., Portage, MI 49024, by telephone at 616-349-4006 or by e-mail at *jo.cornell@wmich.edu*

Cheryl Costello-Forshey is a writer and poet whose poems appear in other *Chicken Soup for the Soul* books. She is in the process of finding a publisher for her first book of poems. Meanwhile, she is busy working on her second book. She also writes commissioned pieces for any occasion or for no particular occasion at all. If you are interested in having Cheryl write a personalized poem for someone in your life, or if you would like to contact her for any other reason, she can be reached at 36240 S. 16th Rd., Barnesville, OH 43713 or by calling 740-757-9217.

Joseph Danziger is an attorney. He and his wife, Randi, have one daughter, Jillian, a twenty-year-old junior at Penn State University. Joe's story, "A Dad's Change of Life" was written the evening following the day he and his wife dropped off their daughter at Penn State to begin her college experience.

Gunter David was born in Berlin, Germany and moved to the United States at age eighteen to study journalism. Gunter's first career was as a reporter on major city newspapers for twenty-five years, including the *Evening Bulletin* of Philadelphia, which nominated him for a Pulitzer Prize. Gunter obtained a master's degree in family therapy from Hahnemann University and Medical School in Philadelphia. He recently retired from Johnson & Johnson, where he served in the employee assistance program as family therapist and addiction counselor to employees and their families. Since retirement, he has become a published author of fiction and nonfiction. In 1997, he won first prize in the literary short-story category at the annual Philadelphia Writers Conference.

Mary J. Davis began writing when the "empty nest" syndrome hit. She also enrolled in college and earned two bachelor's degrees. Mary writes magazine articles, short stories, Christian stories for children and teens, as well as Sunday school curriculum, devotions and greeting cards. Mary's thirty books have been published by Rainbow, Legacy and Shining Star. She speaks at Christian Education Seminars, ladies' groups and children's rallies. Mary also presents writing workshops for children. Mary and her husband, Larry, have three grown children. She can be reached at P.O. Box 27, Montrose, IA 52639.

Kathy Johnson Gale knew even as a freshman at U.C.L.A. that she would someday be a writer. Her work has been published in numerous national magazines and anthologies, including *Guideposts' Best Loved Stories* and the Institute of Children's Literature Success Stories for the '90s. Also as a freshman, she met her husband. They now live in Frankfort, Kentucky and are the parents of three daughters, the oldest a college graduate and the two youngest in college.

Zan Gaudioso is a freelance writer whose stories have appeared in newspapers across the country. Zan earned her degree in special education for the deaf and went on to teach sign language, as well as teaching deaf children and adults. She became part of a landmark program that was the first to utilize sign language in order to foster verbal language skills in autistic children. From there, with additional training, she went on to become a surgical nurse. With writing as an integral driving force in her life, she continued to write and be published in newspapers and in family medical journals. She is presently negotiating with a major network to bring to television a one-hour drama based on her true life story. She currently lives with her fiancé and their dog, Delilah, in Santa Monica, California. She can be reached at *justzan@usa.net*

Randy Glasbergen has had more than twenty-five thousand cartoons published in magazines, books and greeting cards around the world. He also creates *The Better Half*, which is syndicated to newspapers by King Features Syndicate. You can find more of Randy's cartoons online at *www.glasbergen.com*

Miriam Goldstein's body cast now resides in her basement, slowly dissolving under the combined assault of dampness and insects. However, Miriam herself has no plans for dissolution in the immediate future. She is a native of Manchester, New Hampshire and is currently attending Brown University, where she is double-majoring in biology and English. She enjoys wandering through tide pools, swamps and woods, haphazardly hammering bits of wood together as a theater techie, making sounds that vaguely resemble music on the flute and tenor sax, meeting unconventional people, and tweaking the nose of popular culture. She despises conformity and intolerance. She can be reached by writing c/o Martin's Associates, 817 Elm St., Manchester, NH 03104 or by e-mail at *khory@juno.com*

Arlene Green is a thirty-one-year-old mother of four boys, all of whom are brilliant and handsome. She lives in Northern California with her family, two dogs and numerous cats. She is a computer programmer by trade and a mommy by profession.

Scott Greenberg is a nationally recognized motivational speaker, humorist and leadership-training consultant. He is also the author of the popular *Jump Start Leadership Workbook* series for students. Each year Scott works with thousands of people at schools, businesses and associations. He can be reached at 800-450-0432 or by e-mail at *ScottGree@aol.com*

Cynthia Hamond is a freelance children's writer. This is her third story for *Chicken Soup for the Soul*. Cynthia volunteers at St. Henry's as a teacher, lecturer and visits the homebound. She enjoys her school visits and answering her e-mail from readers. She can be reached at 1021 W. River St., Monticello, MN 55362 or by e-mail at *Candbh@aol.com*

Stephen Hopson has been deaf since birth. He graduated from Marist College with a B.S. in business/finance in 1982. After working on Wall Street for fifteen years, he is now a highly acclaimed inspirational speaker. He has spoken to thousands of corporations, colleges and associations about his humorous and inspiring journey in the pursuit of what his mother once told him were "pie-in-the-sky dreams." Stephen specializes in teaching people his unique formula for success through the willingness to take risks, the ability to change and the willingness to accept ourselves as spiritual beings having a human experience. Stephen will be coauthoring *Chicken Soup for the Challenged Soul* (working title) about people with disabilities. His first book, *The Possibilities Are Deafening*, will be released in late 1999 or early 2000. To schedule him for a power-packed presentation, contact your favorite speaker's bureau or the Chicken Soup for the Soul Speaker's Bureau at 805-563-2935, ext. 12. He can be reached directly at 35820 Jefferson Ave., Ste. 206, Harrison Township, MI 48045, by fax at 734-629-0480, or by e-mail at *sjhopson@ibm.net*

John Javna is an innovative and irreverent thinker whose books constantly break the mold of what an author, editor and publisher should be. His instinct for trends is impressive and his output has been both prodigious and popular. Since 1983, Javna has written, edited, created and/or published over fifty books. His *50 Simple Things You Can Do to Save the Earth*, the first book published under his own Earth Works imprint, was on the *New York Times* bestseller list in 1990 for thirty-two weeks—at #1 for seventeen of them—and has sold over 3.5 million copies. Javna's next book, *50 Simple Things Kids Can Do to Save the Earth*, stayed on the *Times* list for eleven weeks and sold 1 million copies. As for the ten books in the *Uncle John's Bathroom Readers* series—published yearly since 1988 by Javna's other imprint, Bathroom Readers' Press—sales have not only passed the 2 million mark, but have spawned a host of imitators and legitimized an entirely new book genre.

Paul Karrer has published over fifty articles and short stories. His story "The Babyflight" had over 300,000 copies published in *A 4th Course of Chicken Soup for the Soul*. He has taught in Western Samoa, Korea, England, Connecticut and currently teaches in California. He can be reached at 457 Archer St., Monterey, CA or by e-mail at *pkarrer123@yahoo.com*

Will Keim holds a Ph.D. in higher education with an emphasis in college student services administration from the Oregon State University. He completed his B.A. and M.A. in speech communication at the University of the Pacific in

California. A four-year varsity letterman in baseball, Will has been selected as an Outstanding Young Man of America, Outstanding Professor of the Year, and was awarded the prestigious Durwood Owen Pi Kappa Phi Award for Outstanding Interfraternalism. Dr. Keim has lectured personally on over one thousand campuses across North America and has spoken directly to 2 million college and university students from every state in the U.S. and several provinces in Canada. His corporate clients include Delta Air Lines, AT&T, IBM, State Farm Insurance, Rotary International and the National Employer's Council. Dr. Keim is married to Donna and the father of four children. He resides with his family in Corvallis, Oregon.

April Kemp, M.S., is an award-winning motivational speaker and sales trainer. She is dynamic with a high-energy delivery style dedicated to the education of audiences nationwide. Along with her husband, April developed a motivational software product, "Motivational Mind Bytes." She can be reached at 800-307-8821.

Brandon Lagana is assistant director of admissions at Ball State University in Muncie, Indiana and is cofounder of the Student Association for Volunteer Opportunities at West Chester University, in West Chester, Pennsylvania. Over the past eleven years, he has combined creatively his love of music and volunteering by performing at numerous churches, nursing homes and prisons throughout Delaware and Pennsylvania.

Jeanne Marie Laskas publishes essays and articles in numerous national magazines, including *Esquire, GQ, Allure, Good Housekeeping, Glamour, Redbook, Reader's Digest* and others. Her column, *Significant Others*, appears weekly in the *Washington Post* magazine, and focuses on the trials of tribulations of relationships in the 1990's. Her first book, *The Balloon Lady and Other People I Know* (Duquesne University Press, 1996), is a collection of essays and stories, and her second, *We Remember* (Morrow, 1999), is a series of stories about one-hundred-year-old ladies looking back on the century. A professor of creative nonfiction in the graduate writing program at Goucher College in Baltimore, Jeanne Marie has an M.F.A. in nonfiction writing from the University of Pittsburgh, and a B.A. from St. Joseph's University in Philadelphia. She is currently working on her third book, *Fifty Acres and a Poodle* (Bantam, 1999), about life on her farm in Scenery Hill, Pennsylvania with her husband, three dogs, horse and a mule.

Lisa Levenson graduated from the University of Pennsylvania in 1997. She was editorial-page editor of the *Daily Pennsylvanian,* house manager of her sorority, Phi Sigma Sigma, and a member of the university team that appeared on the MSNBC game show *Remember This?* During college, Lisa also wrote for the commentary page of the *Philadelphia Inquirer.* A Pittsburgh native, she is currently a management consultant and freelance writer in Washington, D.C. She can be reached at *lisalevenson@usa.net*

Eric Linder graduated from the University of Florida after five years of friendship, late-night pizza and football games. He currently is teaching outdoor education to children in Dahlonega, Georgia. He enjoys laughing, spontaneity and thinking about "matters of consequence."

Sarah Lockyer was born and raised in Toronto, Ontario and has been writing for most of her life. She is currently enjoying a year off from school, but plans to attend a university in the future, majoring in journalism. She plays guitar and writes a lot of poetry in her spare time and loves to travel. She can be reached at 416-281-1707.

Paula Lopez-Crespin lives in Denver, Colorado and is a wife and the mother of two children. "I Passed the Test" is her first published work. She hopes to have several of her children's books and a novel published soon.

Tony Luna is founder of Tony Luna Creative Services, a creative consultancy, as well as cofounder of New Media Marketplace, a digital production service. He is also an instructor at the Art Center College of Design in the field of creativity and business. Tony is a member of the board of directors of U.P., Inc. a nonprofit organization that encourages young people to enter education and employment in the entertainment industry. He can be reached at 819 North Bel Aire Dr., Burbank, CA 91501.

Elsa Lynch is a single parent currently residing in Missouri. She graduated from Virginia Wesleyan College in Norfolk, Virginia. Elsa recently left her position in customer service and is planning to take the plunge into full-time freelance writing. She can be reached at *Elsa@socket.net*

Hanoch McCarty, Ed.D., is a highly sought-after motivational speaker whose corporate training programs focus on strategies that build employee and customer loyalty, as well as freeing creativity and maximizing personal productivity. His work uses the bottom-line power of kindness and integrity. He can be reached at Learning Resources, P.O. Box 66, Galt, CA 95632, via e-mail at *kindness@bigfoot.com*, or by phone at 209-745-2212.

Robert Tate Miller is an internationally published writer who has also worked as a television promotions writer/producer. He has written four screenplays and a number of essays on his early years growing up in a small North Carolina mountain town. He can be reached at 950 Highland Ave., Los Angeles, CA 90024.

Beth Mullally is the editorial-page editor and a columnist for the *Times Herald-Record* in Middletown, New York. She is also a regular contributor to *Reader's Digest* and author of the book the *Best of Beth*, a collection of her columns. She and her husband, Bob Quinn, have two sons, two dogs, two cars, two televisions—and two mortgages. She can be reached at (914) 346-3181 or by e-mail at *bmullally@th-record.com*

Megan Narcini transferred from Virginia Tech to the College of New Jersey in January 1999 to major in nursing. Although she has been writing since her early teens, this is her first published work. She would like to thank her family, friends and her high school creative writing teacher, Ms. Olsen, for supporting her dream to write. She can be reached by e-mail at *tigereyz@theglobe.com*

Kristi Nay really enjoyed attending Westmont College (a Christian college in Santa Barbara, California). She majored in English literature because of her love of reading and writing, which she inherited from her family. She graduated in 1983, but later returned to Westmont to get her teaching credential, and then taught for four years at the Santa Ynez Valley Christian Academy.

She left teaching to start of private, nonprofit bed and breakfast in 1989, called Shepherds' Keep, for tired Christian pastors and their wives. She and her husband Steve now operate Shepherds' Keep in Colorado. They have been married fourteen years but didn't meet until they had both graduated from their respective colleges. (He attended Fresno Pacific whose basketball team is a rival of Westmont's). Steve is a technical writer and, hence, makes a great editor for Kristi's pastime of writing. She can be reached at *GoodPirate@aol.com*

Kent Nerburn is an author, sculptor and educator who has been deeply involved in Native American issues and education. He has served as project director for two books of oral history, entitled *To Walk the Red Road* and *We Choose to Remember*. He has also edited three highly acclaimed books on Native American subjects. Kent won the Minnesota Award for his book, *Neither Wolf Nor Dog: On Forgotten Roads in 1995*. Kent holds a Ph.D. in theology and art and lives with his family in Bemidju, Minnesota.

Vicki Niebrugge has successfully combined academics with the corporate and association arena. She is an associate professor at Cleary College of Business in Ann Arbor, Michigan, teaching in the management department. She is also an internationally recognized speaker, trainer, author and consultant with the NOVA Group. She holds a B.A. and M.A. from Eastern Michigan University and a J.D. from the University of Toledo.

Dorri Olds is an illustrator and graphic designer in New York City. She illustrated the children's book, *Irving Goes to Town* (PPC Books), and book covers for Avalon Books. Her design work includes brochures, newsletters, logos and books. Ms. Olds's paintings have been exhibited in numerous New York City galleries and private collections.

Varda One is a self-explorer who translates her discoveries into essays, poems, short stories, plays, novels, songs and pamphlets, many of which have been published worldwide. Her hobbies include reinventing herself by doing the impossible; her values are growth, enjoyment and usefulness. Her work also appears in *A 4th Course of Chicken Soup for the Soul.*

Kevin Randall has been a leadership trainer and public speaker for the past seven years, having spoken at the National Association for Campus Activities National Convention, NACA Great Lakes Regional Conference, and to high school students across Michigan. In 1997, Kevin developed his most requested presentation, entitled Leadership as a Lifestyle, and has presented this session to rave reviews at high schools, colleges and conferences nationwide. For more information about Kevin Randall or his leadership programs contact, *Randallkev@hotmail.com*

Eva Rosenberg, M.B.A., E.A., affectionately known as "TaxMama" to her tax clients and fans, writes a weekly newsletter, *Ask TaxMama*. She is a moderator of the Internet's *HelpDesk*, a popular speaker on tax, marketing and Internet topics, and the visionary behind the world's first universal gift registry, My Wish List. Visit her at *http://taxmama.com*

Christa F. Sandelier received a B.S. in horticulture from Delaware Valley College in 1996 and an M.S. in counseling from Shippensburg University in 1999. She is originally from Clayton, New Jersey and currently is a residence director at Shippensburg University.

Richard Santana , Ed.M, was born in California and became the third generation of his family to join one of the largest gangs in California. After several
years of hate, drugs, and violence on the streets, he experienced a transformation, which he credits to education. In 1995, Richard graduated from the
Harvard University Graduate School of Education, Human Development and
Psychology. He offers a valuable opportunity to understand the complexities
of diversity in the workplace, schools and communities. For more information,
call 510-336-1780 or e-mail him at *mr.chocolate@earthlink.net*

Adam Saperston is an emergency medicine physician who loves sharing stories about life and transformation. He has had the privilege and opportunity
to make a difference by speaking at universities and high schools. He is currently completing a book about his experiences as an ER resident and student.

Eric Saperston has spent the last six years traveling the country in a 1971
Volkswagen bus with three of his friends, a golden retriever and a video cam-
era. The purpose of their travels is to bridge the generation gap and open up
a dialogue between those in our country who want to learn and those who
want to teach. Currently, they have captured 380 hours of footage and have
interviewed over 175 of our nation's greatest teachers such as former
President Jimmy Carter, actor Henry Winkler, musician Jerry Garcia, Olympic
gold medallist Carl Lewis and astronaut Kathy Thornton. Eric and his team
are currently making a film with Walt Disney Studios about their adventures,
writing a book and on a national speaking tour. "The Journey," as it's known,
can be reached by calling 805-377-7378 or by e-mail at *Pushthebus@aol.com*

Harley Schwadron is a self-taught cartoonist living in Ann Arbor, Michigan,
who worked as a journalist and public relations writer before switching to
cartooning full-time in 1984. His cartoons appear in *Barron's, Harvard Business
Review,* the *Wall Street Journal, National Law Journal* and many others. He can be
reached at P.O. Box 1347, Ann Arbor, MI 48106 or by calling 313-426-8433.

Cynthia Stewart-Copier is a successful business owner, author and speaker.
She has had the opportunity to speak to audiences around the world. She is
an important story contributor to the *New York Times* bestselling holiday book,
Christmas Miracles, and appeared in December with Barbara Walters on *The
View.* Cynthia and her story were a featured part of a half-hour segment
devoted to the book. She will have two stories in the forthcoming book,
Mother's Miracles. She has had many stories published, with the most recent in
Dreambuilders magazine, a magazine for successful business owners. Cynthia's
newest book, *Dreams of My Own* (Internet, April 1999), was inspired after
attending Mark Victor Hansen's and Jack Canfield's seminar, "How to Build a
Speaking and Writing Empire."

B. T. Thomas was educated in the Philadelphia school systems. She was married to Ronald Mark Thomas and has one daughter, Stacee Marie (Thomas)
Nettles. She is "Mom-Mom" to two lovely grandchildren, Ronald Marc and
Morgan Alexis. She completed her masters of ministry in biblical studies and
has now received her doctor of divinity from the Jameson School of
International Ministries. B. T. has been involved in international missions
since 1982. She has two self-published books, *From the Heart of a Blessed Temple*

and *Grandma's Quilt: Her Stories and Ours*. She has taken early retirement to pursue her writing and missions endeavors.

JeVon Thompson has been one of America's premier power speakers since 1980. A member of "Who's Who in American Colleges and Universities" and a recipient of the 1974 Merit Award, JeVon is a Milton College graduate with a B.A. in psychology. As a musician, he worked with Handy Award winner Luther Allison and completed a student apprenticeship with the Duke Ellington Band. His lectures and seminars on personal power span across the United States, Canada and throughout the Caribbean. He has been featured on ABC's *All My Children*, a nationally televised Oprah Winfrey special with Michael Jordan, and hosted a Tele-Link special, *Keep Our World Tobacco Free*. He is the producer of four educational videos, including the national bestseller, *Waking Up from Dope*. His writing credits include the novel *Crutches* and co-authorship of *Teen Power Too*.

Rosa Torcasio resides in Norwalk, Connecticut. She is a junior at the University of Connecticut where she majors in human development and family relations. Her career goal is to work with less fortunate children and allow them the opportunities to advance both academically and socially. She enjoys reading and spending time with her family: her parents, Francesco and Antonia, and also her sister, Serafina, and her brother, Vincenzo. She would like to dedicate this article to her Nonna Serafina: "Grazie per tutto Nonna— mi manchi tanto e ti voglio tanto bene." Rosa can be reached by e-mail at *MammaRo@aol.com* or *BellezzaRo@aol.com*

Glenn Van Ekeren is a dynamic speaker and trainer dedicated to assisting people and organizations in maximizing their potential. Glenn is the author of *Speakers Sourcebook, Speaker's Sourcebook II* and the *Popular Potential Newsletter*. Glenn has a wide variety of written publications and audio and video presentations available. He can be reached at People Building Institute, 330 Village Circle, Sheldon, IA 51201 or by calling 800-899-4878.

Kevin Van Gundy is an international business consultant and professional speaker who helps companies create and care for customers. Currently, Kevin sits on the board of several companies and is actively involved with the start-up of two others. He lives in Grand Junction, Colorado, with his wife Lauryn and their four children. In 1996, he was selected by the U.S. Government-funded Citizens Democracy Corp to travel to the former Eastern Bloc country of Bulgaria to start one of its first advertising agencies. Kevin is a recent graduate of the Masters in Public Administration Program at the Colorado University at Denver. He is deeply involved in politics and has already run for public office twice. His focus is on the subject of generativity and he spends a great deal of his time motivating young people to become involved in the American political system and to vote! He is in the final stages of writing his first book, *Titanic: An American Allegory*, which is scheduled to be published in fall 1999 by Pendant Publishing, Inc.

Tal Vigderson was born in San Diego, California. Tal has an undergraduate degree in film from San Diego State University with distinction in his major. He has had careers in photography, entertainment marketing research and teaching in several grade levels, including special education in a junior high school in south central Los Angeles. Tal attended law school at Loyola of Los

Angeles and passed the California Bar. He is currently working as an entertainment attorney in Los Angeles representing filmmakers, writers, directors, producers, Internet companies and major studios in various forms of transactional work. Tal likes to travel and enjoys tennis, hiking and photography. He can be reached at *TOV3@aol.com*

Daneen Kaufman Wedekind is from Bridge City, Texas. She enjoys writing and is a columnist for an online parenting magazine, *All Mixed Up*. A mother, a nurse and a writer, Daneen finds the greatest joy in her children, Kristofer and Kameron. She considers the two most precious gifts in her life to be the hugs of her children and the written word. She gives special thanks to God for the ability to write, and to Mark for the ability to love again.

Joan Wiberg is a cartoonist and illustrator living in the Washington, D.C. metropolitan area. Her cartoons have been published in national magazines for adults and children.

David Wiemers is a writer and producer of many of your favorite television shows, including *Major Dad, Harry and the Hendersons* and *DuckTales*. A member of the National Speakers' Association, he's also a humorist who gives hundreds of presentations yearly. He can be reached by e-mail at *infoplus@earthlink.net*

Permissions

We would like to acknowledge the following publishers and individuals for permission to reprint the following material. (Note: The stories that were penned anonymously, that are in the public domain, or that were written by Jack Canfield, Mark Victor Hansen, Kimberly Kirberger or Dan Clark are not included in this listing.)

Common Ground. Reprinted by permission of Megan Narcini. ©1999 Megan Narcini.

Never Say Never. Reprinted by permission of Rosa Torcasio. ©1999 Rosa Torcasio.

College Bound. Reprinted by permission of Dave Barry. ©1998 Dave Barry.

Bloopers from College Admission Essays. Reprinted by permission of Richard Lederer. ©1999 Richard Lederer.

Strange Scholarships. Reprinted from *Uncle John's Great Big Bathroom Reader* by The Bathroom Readers' Institute. Copyright ©1998 by Bathroom Readers' Press, *www.bathroomreader.com* Reprinted with permission.

The Envelope, Please, written by Rory Evans. Copyright ©1995, *Seventeen* magazine. Reprinted by permission of the *Los Angeles Times.*

If the Dream Is Big Enough, the Facts Don't Count. Reprinted by permission of Cynthia Stewart-Copier. ©1999 Cynthia Stewart-Copier.

Hani. Reprinted by permission of Jamie Winship. ©1999 Jamie Winship.

Inspiration Can Be Anywhere. Reprinted by Cerie L. Couture. ©1999 Cerie L. Couture.

A Proposal to Myself. Reprinted by permission of Sarah Lockyer. ©1999 Sarah Lockyer.

Good-Bye, Mr. Blib; Breakdown of Family Traced to Psych. 1 Student and *College Wisdom Seldom Exercised in the Summer.* Reprinted by permission of Beth Mullally. ©1999 Beth Mullally.

A Dad Says Good-Bye. Reprinted by permission of Joseph Danziger. ©1999 Joseph Danziger.

The "No-Hug" Rule. Reprinted by permission of Cheryl Costello-Forshey. ©1999 Cheryl Costello-Forshey.

Shoes in the Shower. Reprinted by permission of Lia Gay and Rebecca Hart. ©1999 Lia Gay and Rebecca Hart.

Deck the Halls, written by Melanie Fester. Copyright ©1995, *Seventeen* magazine. Reprinted by permission of the *Los Angeles Times.*

The Times I Called Home from College. Reprinted by permission of Scott Greenberg. ©1999 Scott Greenberg.

The Long Road Home. Reprinted by permission of Lia Gay. ©1999 Lia Gay.

Undeclared. Reprinted by permission of Tal Vigderson. ©1999 Tal Vigderson.

Stuck with No Way Out. Reprinted by permission of Rosanne Martorella. ©1999 Rosanne Martorella.

A Better Message. Reprinted by permission of Carol Grace Anderson, M.A. ©1999 Carol Grace Anderson, M.A.

Homeboy Goes to Harvard. Reprinted by permission of Richard Santana. ©1999 Richard Santana.

From the Heart of a Blessed Temple. Reprinted by permission of B. T. Thomas. ©1999 B. T. Thomas.

Second Kind of Mind. Reprinted by permission of JeVon Thompson. ©1999 JeVon Thompson.

Work for Your Supper. Reprinted by permission of Arlene Green. ©1999 Arlene Green.

Catsup Soup. Reprinted by permission of Cynthia Hamond. ©1999 Cynthia Hamond.

Student Super-Saver™. Reprinted by permission of Kevin Van Gundy. ©1999 Kevin Van Gundy.

Dare to Take Risks! Reprinted by permission of Stephen Hopson. ©1999 Stephen Hopson.

All in the Family. Reprinted by permission of Jeanne Marie Laskas. ©1999 Jeanne Marie Laskas.

Life Lessons. Reprinted by permission of Dave Barry. ©1997 Dave Barry.

A Homecoming of a Different Sort. Reprinted by permission of Vicki Niebrugge. ©1999 Vicki Niebrugge.

Two Stories for Life. Reprinted by permission of Robert Fulghum. ©1999 Robert Fulghum.

Humor Them! Reprinted by permission of Katherine D. Ortega. ©1999 Katherine D. Ortega.

Know Where You're Going! From *Speaker's Sourcebook II* by Glenn Van Ekeren Copyright ©1994. Reprinted with permission of Prentice Hall Direct: A Division of Arco.

Improving Your Life Every Day

Real people sharing real stories — for nineteen years. Now, Chicken Soup for the Soul has gone beyond the bookstore to become a world leader in life improvement. Through books, movies, DVDs, online resources and other partnerships, we bring hope, courage, inspiration and love to hundreds of millions of people around the world. Chicken Soup for the Soul's writers and readers belong to a one-of-a-kind global community, sharing advice, support, guidance, comfort, and knowledge.

Chicken Soup for the Soul stories have been translated into more than 40 languages and can be found in more than one hundred countries. Every day, millions of people experience a Chicken Soup for the Soul story in a book, magazine, newspaper or online. As we share our life experiences through these stories, we offer hope, comfort and inspiration to one another. The stories travel from person to person, and from country to country, helping to improve lives everywhere.

Share with Us

We all have had Chicken Soup for the Soul moments in our lives. If you would like to share your story or poem with millions of people around the world, go to chickensoup.com and click on "Submit Your Story." You may be able to help another reader, and become a published author at the same time. Some of our past contributors have launched writing and speaking careers from the publication of their stories in our books!

Our submission volume has been increasing steadily — the quality and quantity of your submissions has been fabulous. We only accept story submissions via our website. They are no longer accepted via mail or fax.

To contact us regarding other matters, please send us an e-mail through webmaster@chickensoupforthesoul.com, or fax or write us at:

Chicken Soup for the Soul
P.O. Box 700
Cos Cob, CT 06807-0700
Fax: 203-861-7194

One more note from your friends at Chicken Soup for the Soul: Occasionally, we receive an unsolicited book manuscript from one of our readers, and we would like to respectfully inform you that we do not accept unsolicited manuscripts and we must discard the ones that appear.

Chicken Soup
www.chickensoup.com
for the Soul